Heiner Henninges · Minolta Dynax 8000i

MINOLTA DYNAX 8000i

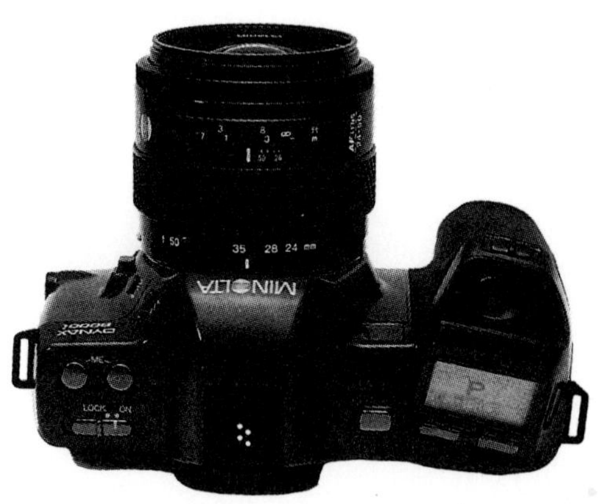

in U.S.A. & Canada

MAXXUM™ 8000i

Heiner Henninges

HOVE FOTO BOOKS

In U.S.A. and Canada

the Minolta Dynax 8000i is known as the

Maxxum 8000i

All text, illustrations and data apply to cameras with either name
U.S.A. Edition ISBN 0-906477-80-1

Minolta Dynax 8000i

First English Edition November 1990
Published by Hove Foto Books
34 Church Road, Hove, Sussex BN3 2GJ

English Translation: Liselotte Sperl
Production Editor: Georgina Fuller
Minolta Technical Advice: Bernard Petticrew
Typesetting & Layout: The Print Box, Brighton BN2 1AE
Printed in Germany by Kösel GmbH, Kempten

British Library Cataloguing in Publication Data
Hennings, Heiner
Minolta Dynax 8000i.
1. 1. 35mm cameras. Techniques
I. Title
771.32

ISBN 0-906447-66-6

UK Distribution

Book Trade:
Fountain Press Ltd.
Queensborough House
Claremont Road
Surbiton, Surrey
KT6 4QU

Photo Trade:
Newpro (UK) Ltd.
Old Sawmills Road
Faringdon, Oxon
SN7 7DS

Contents

Minolta Dynax - The Line of Reason

In the mid 80's Minolta introduced a new era in SLR photography by developing a successful autofocus system: the new Minolta 7000. Functions such as exposure control, film transport and film speed setting had long been automated and accepted by the general public, and now automatic focusing also became a generally-established feature. The autofocus system à la Minolta soon became the standard that other SLR camera manufacturers followed. However, Minolta was not content with the initial success of the 1000-series. It was the aim of the Minolta R&D department to improve their autofocus system even further, to make focusing faster and more reliable and also easier to use. The Minolta autofocus system should not only focus perfectly in reasonable lighting, the aim was also to improve its capabilities in poor light and even in total darkness.

With the introduction of the Dynax series, Minolta have set new standards in the development of autofocus photography. The Minolta Dynax 7000i could be described as the first representative of a new, "intelligent" camera generation. Two further models soon followed: the Dynax 3000i and the Dynax 5000i. The Minolta Dynax 8000i completes the quartet in the Dynax dynasty. This camera is the new flagship of the Dynax series as it opens up the facilities of professional photography to amateur photographers at a price they can afford.

Just like the Dynax 7000i, the 8000i has the same autofocus target area, which can be changed to a

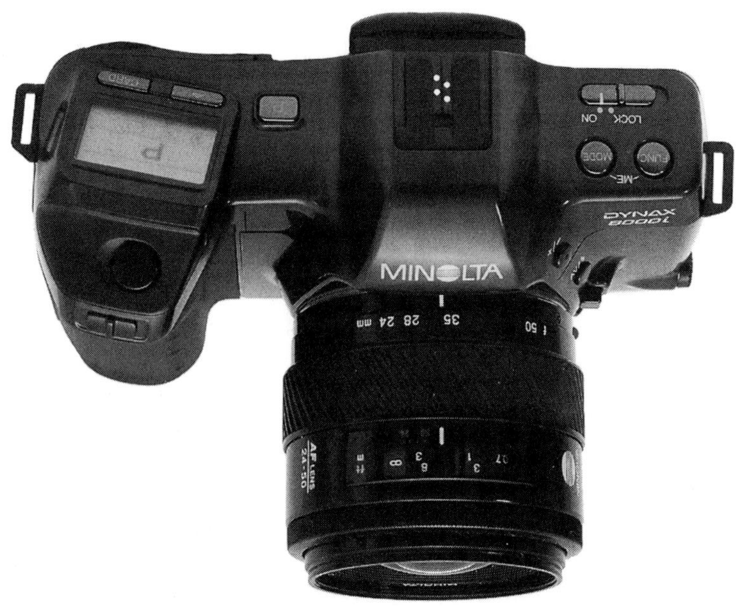

It is a real pleasure to hold the Dynax 8000i – it lies comfortably in your hand because of its ergonomic shape.

smaller one if required. The intelligent autofocus recognizes whether a subject is moving or not and automatically switches from single shot focusing with focus priority to continuous focusing for tracking the moving subject. This predictive autofocus system, introduced for the first time with the Dynax 7000i, is capable of analyzing the movements of a subject and adjusting the focus up to the last fraction of a second before the shutter is released. The Dynax 8000i also has an integrated AF Illuminator to assist the AF system in near or total darkness; the range of this AF Illuminator is specified as 9m by Minolta - however it is possible to focus on even further subjects, depending on available light and subject reflectivity. One new feature on the

8000i is the **FOCUS HOLD** button for interrupting automatic focusing, situated on the camera back to the right of the viewfinder. This function makes automatic focusing easier for subjects that are situated at the edge of the frame and are therefore not covered by the large AF target area at the centre of the frame. With the Customized Function Card it is possible to reprogram the **FOCUS HOLD** button to select the small AF target area at the very centre of the viewfinder screen.

Other new functions, offered on the 8000i, are the super-fast shutter speed of 1/8000 sec and the very fast flash synchronization speed of 1/200 sec which makes fill-in flash even more interesting and precise.

Three modes are available for automatic exposure metering: multi-pattern, centre-weighted average, and spot. When multi-pattern is selected, the exposure mode takes the autofocus data for the main subject into account as well. This means that the subject space, where the main subject is situated, is more strongly considered than the surrounding space.

One special feature of the Dynax 8000i is the multiple exposure facility. If the camera is set to single frame mode, two exposures can be taken on one frame. If the camera is set to continuous shooting, the same frame is continuously exposed as long as the release is kept pressed. A special Creative Expansion card for multiple exposures was developed exclusively for the Dynax 8000i with which it is possible to reprogram this function to your own requirements.

What are the most important features of the Dynax 8000i that make it the ideal camera for the amateur photographer with professional aspirations?

1. Large AF Target Area

The Dynax 8000i utilizes the large AF module, consisting of three metering sensors in an H-shape, which was first introduced with the Dynax 7000i.

2. High Sensitivity AF Sensors

These sensors react even in poor lighting conditions, down to exposure value EV0 at ISO 100/21°. This makes automatic focusing possible in very poor light and increases focusing speed in good light.

3. Predictive Autofocus

The predictive autofocus analyses the movements of the subject, calculating the direction and speed. The focus measurement is continuously adjusted, based on these calculations, right up to the moment the mirror is folded away and the shutter blinds are opened. The change-over from single focusing to continuous focus tracking for moving subjects is automatic.

4. Coupling of Exposure and Distance Metering

The multi-zone exposure metering system, connected with the autofocus system, that has already been so successful in the Dynax 7000i, has also been used in the 8000i. Based on the autofocus data the camera knows where the main subject is situated. It compares the brightness of the main subject and the surrounding picture area to ascertain whether it is uniformly lit or if it is dealing with a backlit subject, or a main subject illuminated by a bright light. Each individual metering area of the silicon photo diode, which is sub-divided into six segments, can be changed in its weighting. The pattern of sensitivity depends on the position of the main subject.

5. Three Metering Methods for Exposure

The Dynax 8000i offers three exposure metering methods; multi-pattern, centre-weighted integral and spot.

6. Intelligent Program Selection

The choice of program mode is automatically made by the focal length of the lens in use at the time. The programs are designed so that, whenever possible, the

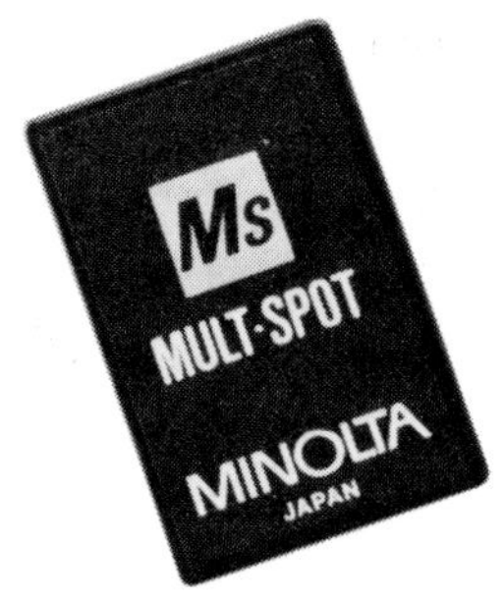

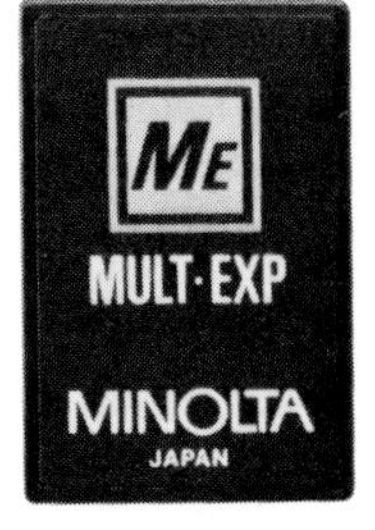

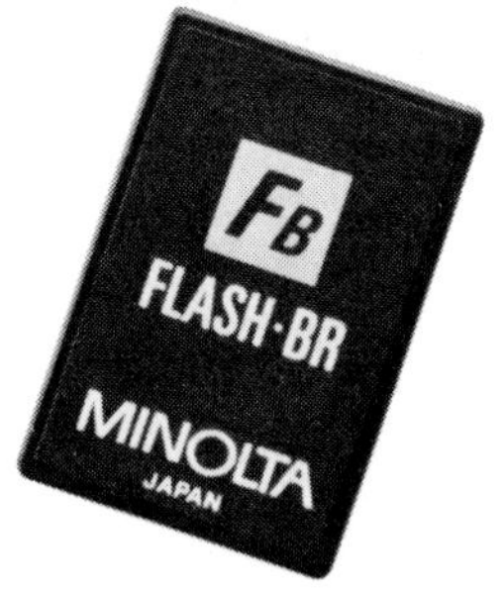

Minolta introduced three new Feature Cards, with the Dynax 8000i, for multi-spot metering, multi-exposures and automatic flash bracketing.

slowest shutter speed is always kept fast enough to permit hand-held shots.

7. Flash Command Mode

Flash exposure is also fully automatic. If Program Flash 5200i, 3200i or 2000i is attached, the Dynax 8000i will automatically switch the flash on when lighting conditions demand. It will also be triggered automatically if the main subject is positioned against a strong back light to provide the right level of fill-in flash.

8. Creative Expansion Card System

The Creative Expansion Card System allows the camera to be programmed and its function extended.

9. Lens System

The range of system lenses offered by Minolta is still the largest for any manufacturer worldwide. Minolta AF lenses distinguish themselves by their excellent quality and compact construction.

10. Compatibility

The Dynax 8000i is compatible with other Minolta autofocus cameras and lenses and is therefore part of the largest and most comprehensive autofocus system in the world.

11. Fastest Shutter Speed

The super-fast shutter speed of 1/8000 sec freezes even the fastest movements. The flash synchronization speed of 1/200 sec facilitates fill-in flash for action shots.

12. Multiple Exposure

The multiple exposure function extends the creative facilities offered by the 8000i. A special Creative Expansion Card provides additional control of this facility.

Good Pictures Right from The Start

It is not necessary to read a manual such as this to produce technically perfect pictures with the Minolta Dynax 8000i. Generally it is quite sufficient to read the instruction manual, fix the carrying strap, insert battery and film, to be ready to take perfectly-exposed and focused pictures.

But if you wish to exploit the many possibilities of this extraordinary camera to realize your own ideas, then you should spend some time getting to know it really well. In addition to the automatic functions, you will be able to use all the other technical facilities offered by the Dynax 8000i if you are fully conversant with them and your fingers can find their way unerringly around the camera.

NAMES OF PARTS

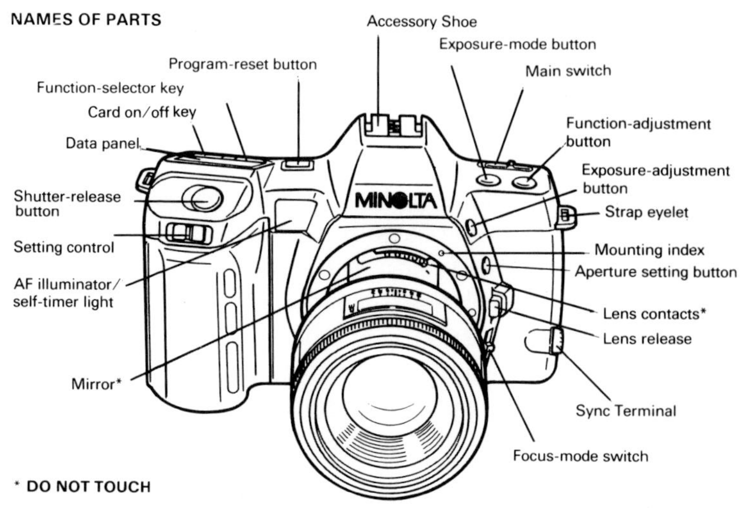

* DO NOT TOUCH

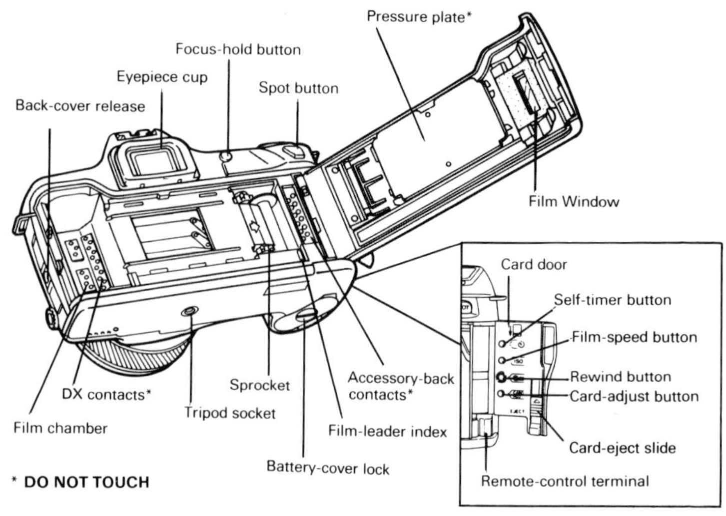

Essential Preparations

All modern, electronically-controlled cameras need a battery to provide the power for their various functions. The Dynax 8000i needs a 6v lithium battery Type 2CR5. It provides the energy for all the camera's functions such as film transport, autofocus and exposure control.

Inserting the battery: With the main switch in the **LOCK** position, insert a coin in the slot of the battery compartment at the base of the handgrip and turn it to **OPEN**. This will release the battery cover and it can be removed. Before inserting the battery, wipe its terminals with a dry cloth to ensure good contact, then insert it according to the marks shown at the top of the compartment. Replace the battery cover and turn the slot to **CLOSE.**

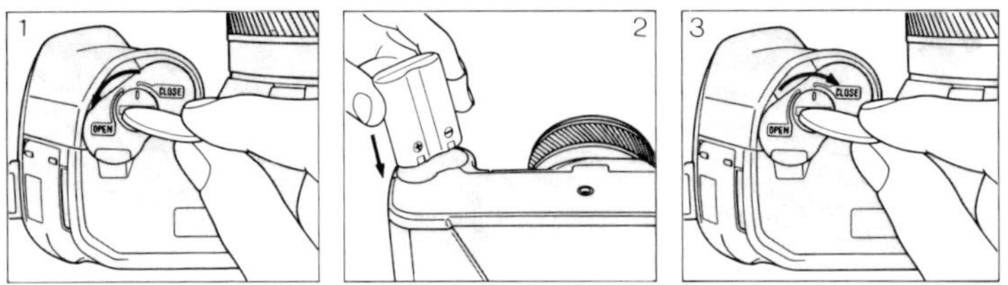

Insert battery: (1) main switch to **LOCK,** insert coin in slot of battery cover, turn to **OPEN,** and remove. (2) clean battery terminals with clean, dry cloth to ensure good contact. Insert lithium battery as indicated. (3) replace cover and lock.

Note: Batteries contain toxic materials that are harmful to the environment. Keep them out of the reach of children. Do not dismantle, recharge, or expose them to high temperatures because they may explode and cause burns. Spent batteries should not be put in the household rubbish but disposed of with special refuse. We recommend that you hand them in at your photographic dealer who will discard them by an environmentally-safe method.

Battery check: Each time the camera is switched on, its computer automatically checks the state of the battery. If the voltage is sufficient then the full-battery symbol will appear for 5 seconds in the LCD panel. If the battery voltage has fallen the low-battery symbol will appear for 5 seconds in the LCD panel and it is a good idea to keep a fresh battery to hand. If the low-battery symbol blinks, while all other displays are still visible, then the battery power is still sufficient to power all functions but it will have to be replaced very soon.

If only the battery symbol blinks or there is no display on the LCD panel at all, then the battery voltage is insufficient for normal operation and the

Fully-charged battery symbol is displayed for five seconds.

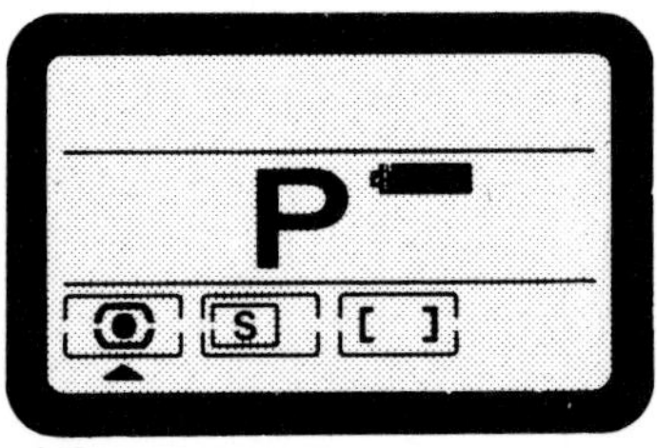

Weak battery symbol is displayed for five seconds: Keep a fresh battery ready.

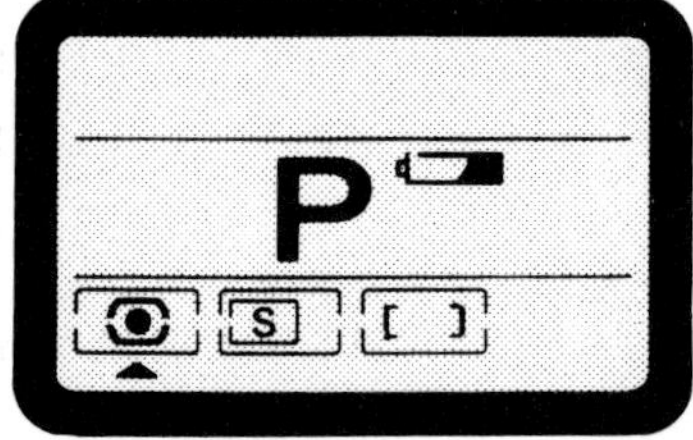

Weak battery symbol flashes: the camera is still functioning but the battery has to be replaced soon.

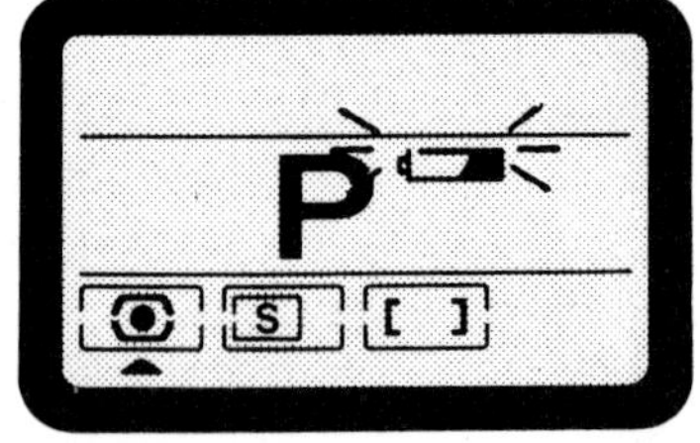

Only the weak battery symbol or no display at all and the release is locked: the voltage of the battery is too low to power any functions, and a new battery has to be inserted immediatly.

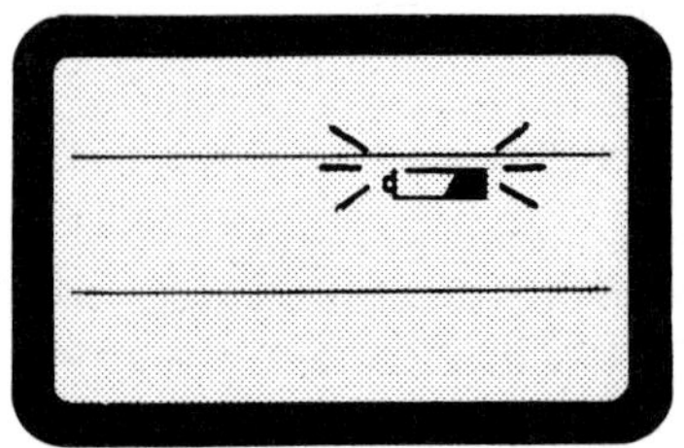

release will be blocked. Now you will have to insert a fresh battery immediately. The audible signal, warning you to insert a new battery, will sound every time the release is pressed while the camera is switched **ON.** If no display is visible, then you should check whether the battery is inserted properly. A fresh battery should be sufficient to expose about 50 x 24-exposure films but the exact number will depend on the actual shooting conditions. Some functions and shooting modes require more energy, some less, and if you use the autofocus facility without actually taking any pictures, the number of exposures will be less. The first battery will almost certainly not produce the above quoted figure as it is only natural - and quite necessary - to experiment as you try to get the feel of the camera and its functions, and this costs quite a lot of energy.

Note: All battery types are adversely affected by low temperatures, i.e. in temperatures below freezing their performance decreases rapidly. Lithium batteries are less affected than some other types of battery but even so it is a good idea to carry the camera close to the body and to keep a spare battery in an inside pocket if you are on a photographic expedition in the cold. Then, if the camera refuses to work properly it can be exchanged for the warm one, but do not discard the first battery as its capacity will be restored in warmer conditions.

Inserting the lens: The major advantage of a SLR camera is that the image on the film is identical to that seen in the viewfinder, and the lenses can be changed to suit any given photographic situation. The bayonet-mount of the Dynax 8000i will accept all lenses with a Minolta AF bayonet. Changing the lens is simple and fast. First remove the body and rear lens caps by turning them counter-clockwise. On the lens and on the camera body are red markers. Align these to fit the lens into the bayonet, then turn it clockwise until it locks into place with a click.

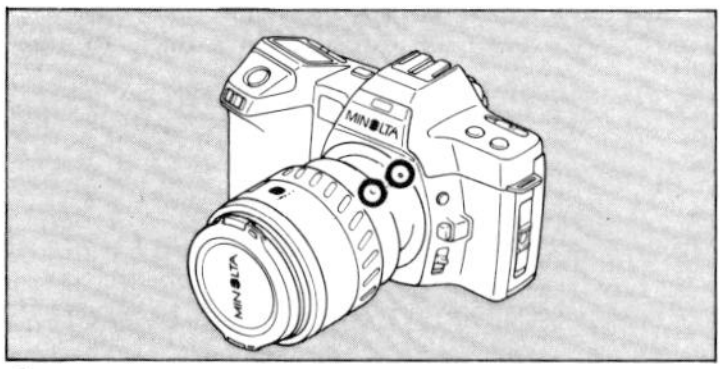

A

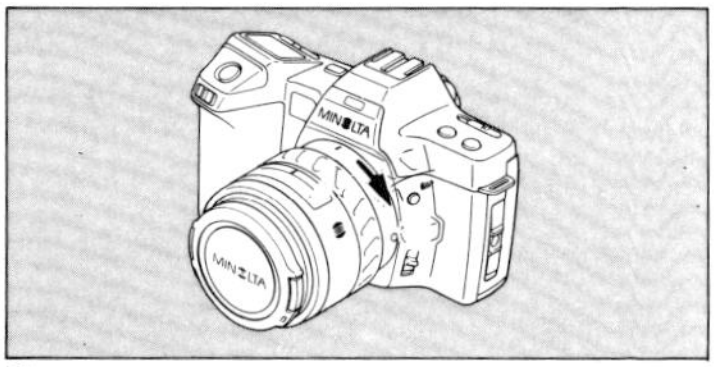

B

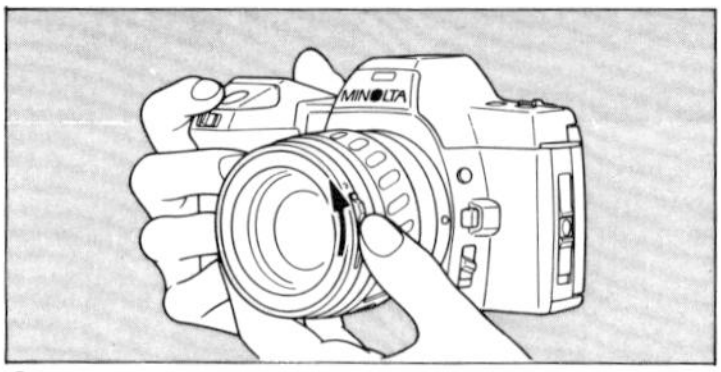

C

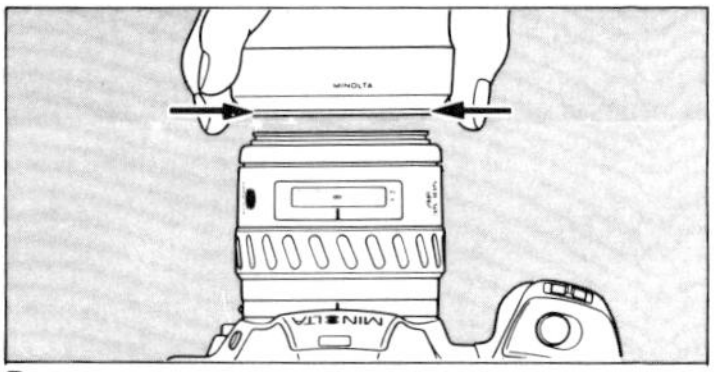

D

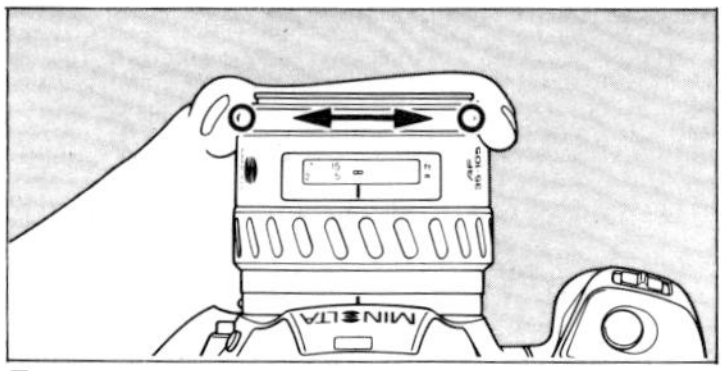

E

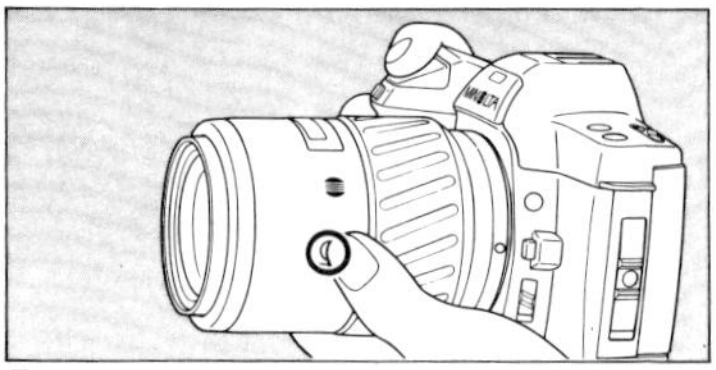

F

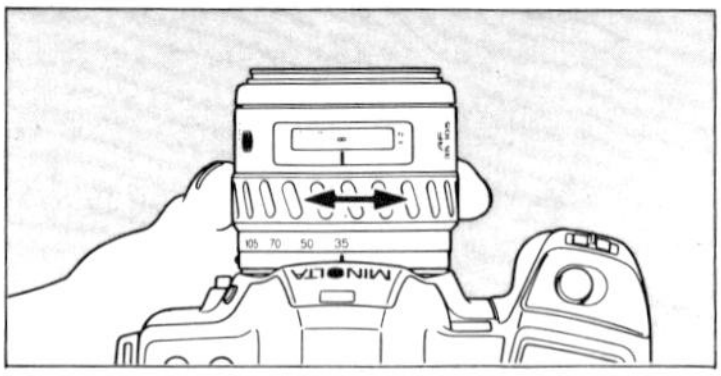

G

First align the red marks on camera and lens (A), the lens can be inserted and locked into position by turning it clockwise (B). Remove the lens cover (C) and fit the lens hood (D). The only other operating elements on the lens are the manual focusing ring (E), the focus-stop button (F) and the zoom ring (G)

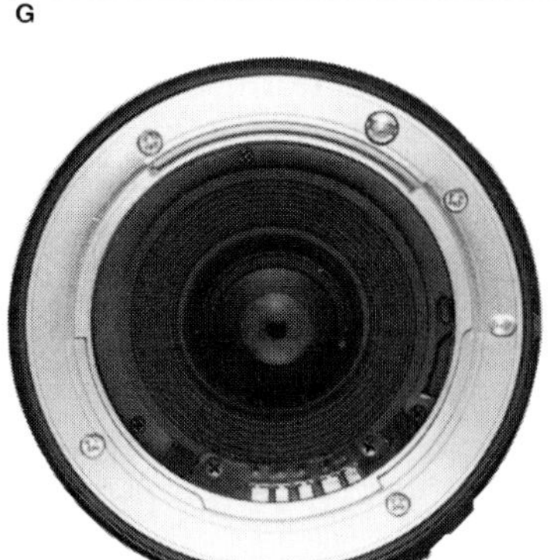

Data flow between the ROM-integrated circuits of lens and camera computer is via five gold contacts.

To remove the lens, press the lens release button and turn the lens counter-clockwise as far as it will go and lift it out.

Note: When changing a lens be careful not to touch any of the contacts, glass surfaces, mirrors, or other interior parts. Always protect the rear element and the camera interior by immediately replacing the body cap and rear lens cap.

Film Loading: Switch the camera on, check that the frame counter shows **0** or no number, and open the back by pressing the button in the centre of the back cover release and sliding the latter downward. Now insert the film cassette into the film chamber, pull the film end out as far as the red marker, making sure it lies flat and the lower row of perforations engage with the teeth of the film transport. Then close the back cover firmly until it clicks shut. The camera will now automatically transport the film forward to the first frame. If the film is correctly loaded the number 1 will appear in the frame counter in the data panel. If it is incorrectly loaded, the **0** will remain in the frame

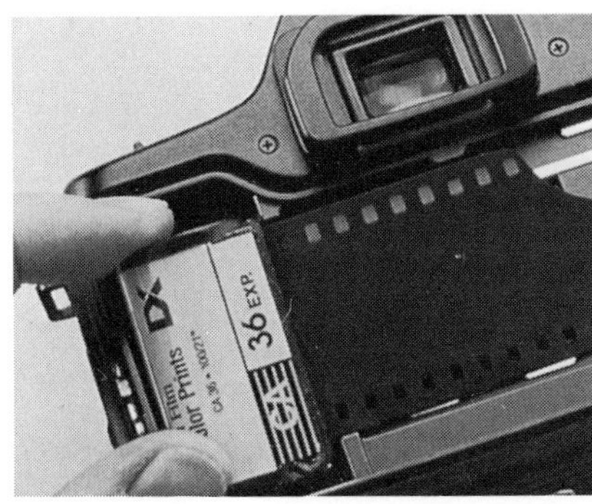

Film loading: the film is automatically engaged in the take-up spool and advanced to the first frame. The film speed is read into the exposure control via the DX-code on the cassette and displayed for about five seconds in the data panel. Incorrect film loading is indicated by the **0** of the frame counter flashing in the data panel.

counter, it will flash and the release is blocked. The camera back has to be opened again and the film loading repeated.

Provided the film is DX-coded, which is the case for most films these days with speeds between ISO 25/15° and 5000/38°, the speed will be read automatically into the exposure control of the camera and displayed on the LCD panel for 5 seconds.

If the loaded film does not have a DX code, then the camera will automatically keep the speed of the last film that was used. If this is incorrect, then the value can be adjusted manually.

Manual setting of film speed is possible in 1/3 stop increments between ISO 25/15° and ISO 6400/39°. Open the card door in the handgrip and press the **FILM-SPEED** button marked **ISO**. The currently-set film speed will appear in the LCD panel. Push the setting control either to the right, to increase the value, or to the left, to decrease it, until the desired value appears. To return to normal function, press the **ISO** button again. If you wish to check which value is presently programmed, simply press the **ISO** button and check the LCD panel.

A wide-angle zoom such as the Minolta AF 25-50mm, f/4, is an ideal companion on any journey. ⇨

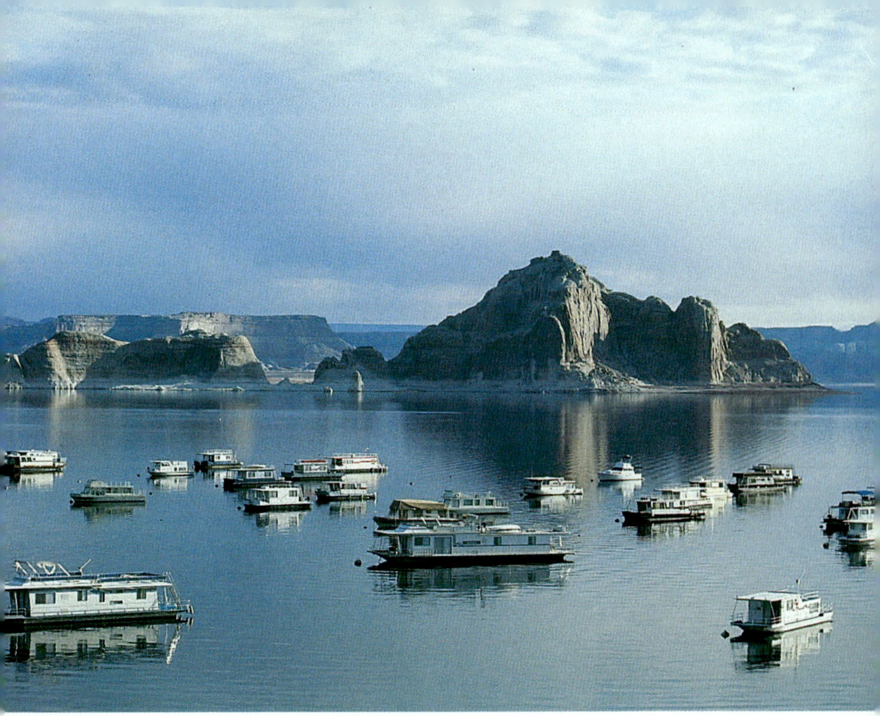

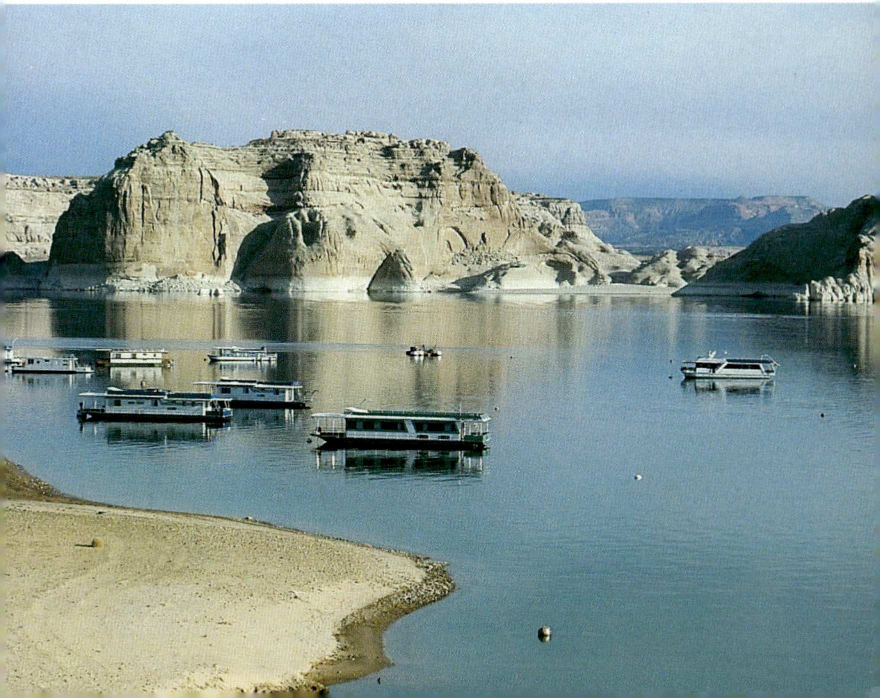

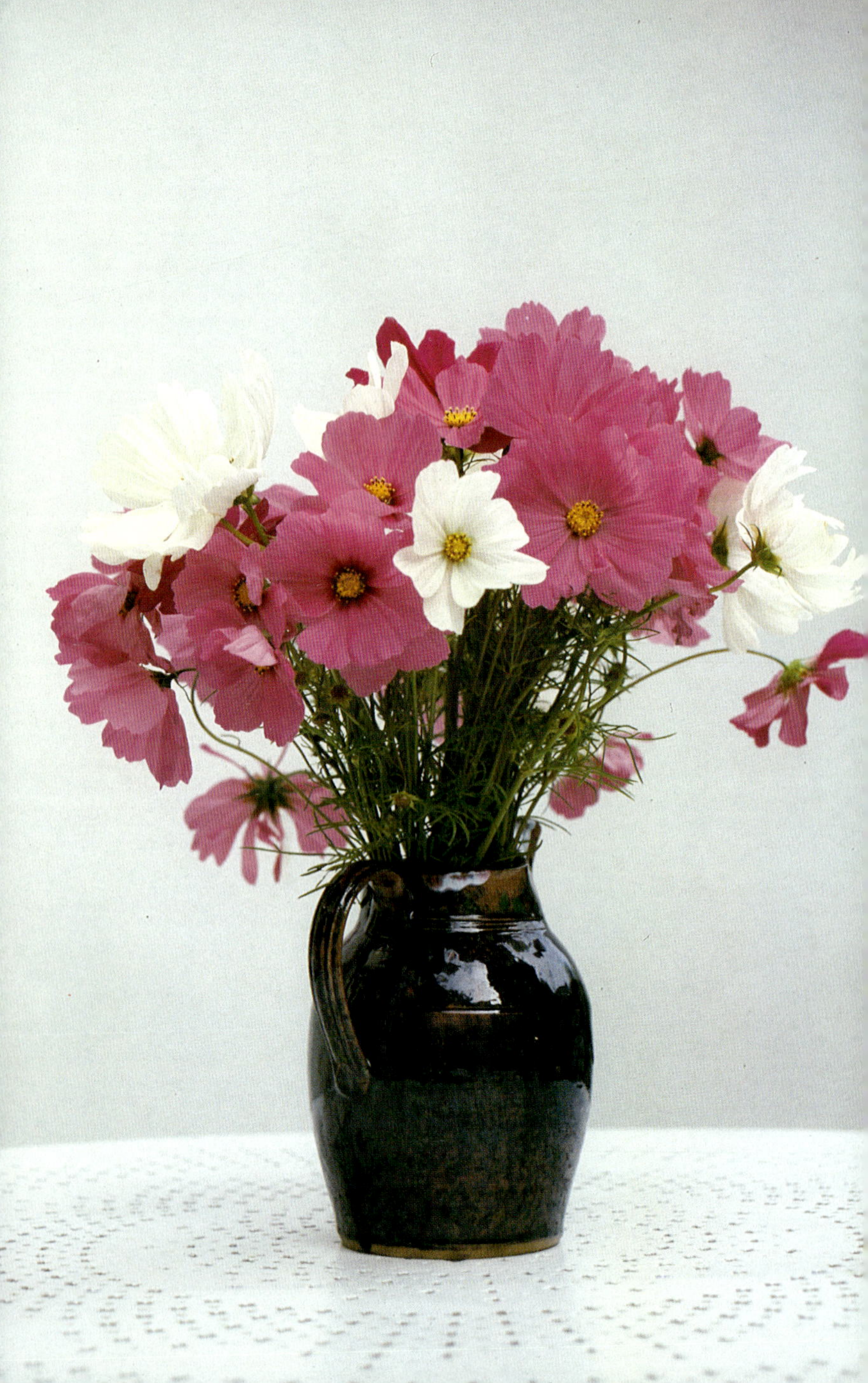

The Dynax 8000i has two automatic film transport modes: Single frame and continuous. In single mode, the film will be exposed one frame at a time. When continuous mode is selected, up to three frames per second will be exposed as long as the release button is held. The focus is continuously adjusted between frames in continuous mode.

To change from single frame to continuous shooting, first press the function-selector key, to move the pointer in the LCD panel to correspond with the symbol for frame advance mode, and then press the function adjustment button, marked **FUNC,** and move the setting control.

Note: Do not touch any delicate parts such as the shutter blind or film pressure plate when loading a film.

Taking Pictures

The film and the battery are loaded, the lens is fitted, so you can start. Slide the main switch to **ON.** Then press the program reset button, marked **P,** which is situated to the left of the data panel, to set the camera for fully automatic operation. Whenever this button is pressed

⇦ *A typical subject for the Highlight / Shadow Control Card. In this case the highlights i.e. the white areas, were measured.*

the camera is set to program exposure mode, autofocus with large metering area, single frame advance, and any exposure compensations are cancelled. This basic setting is the simplest and safest way to obtain perfect snapshots with the Dynax 8000i without having to make any complicated decisions or selecting special settings so this button is therefore sometimes also referred to as the panic button!

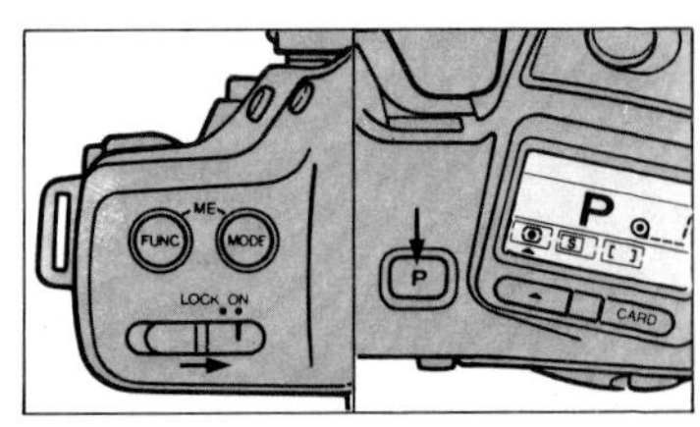

Push main switch **ON,** then press program reset button **P** for fully automatic mode.

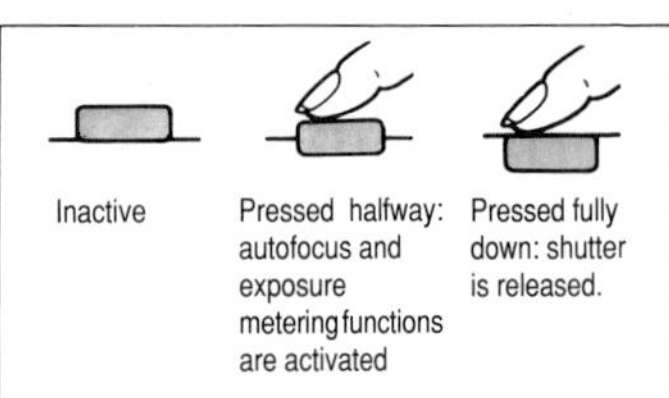

Release positions:

The very bright image in the viewfinder allows assessment of the picture frame and the AF metering area. Point the camera so that the main subject lies within the AF metering area and gently press the release half-way. The camera automatically and rapidly focuses and displays the calculated exposure settings in the viewfinder. If image sharpness is achieved then a green focus signal in the viewfinder will light up. If the red focus signal flashes, automatic focusing is not possible and the lens has to be focused manually.

To take the shot, press the release all the way down firmly but smoothly to avoid camera shake. After the exposure has been made the camera will automatically advance the film to the next frame. The next frame number will appear in the LCD panel.

After the last exposure the camera automatically rewinds the film. This takes about ten seconds for a 36-exposure film and eight seconds for a 24-exposure film. After rewinding, the motor automatically stops and the film cassette symbol in the LCD panel begins to flash, indicating safe removal of film. The frame counter displays a zero. The film is completely rewound into the cassette which prevents confusion between exposed and unexposed films. The release remains locked as long as the rewound film is still in the film chamber. In case the battery voltage was insufficient to rewind the film completely and the battery has to be changed, then the rewinding can be recommenced after changing the battery by pressing the rewind button, situated in the card door. Some photographers prefer the film leader to be left out of the cassette when the film is rewound, as this makes it easier to pull the film from the cassette for processing. This is possible if you are using the Customized Function Card, which is one of the Creative Expansion Cards for the Dynax 8000i and described later.

The camera back should not be opened during or before rewinding. If you accidentally open the back, close it as quickly as possible, so that only a few frames are lost. If rewinding has started before the back is opened, it can only be resumed after the film rewind button has been pressed.

Partially-exposed films may be rewound at any time by opening the card door and pressing the rewind button.

VIEWFINDER

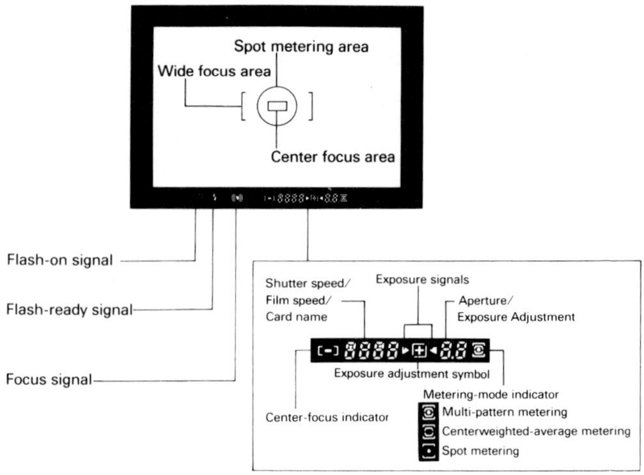

DATA PANEL

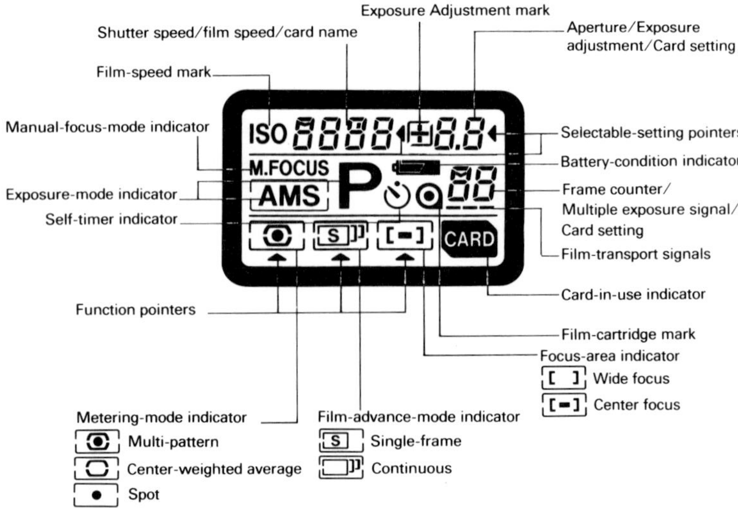

What has been outlined so far is quite sufficient to take good pictures with the Dynax 8000i, but if you are merely satisfied with good pictures, then you need not have invested in a Dynax 8000i. Anyone who is using their Dynax only in the, admittedly, very safe and convenient P mode, may be compared with the driver of a Ferrari, the ultimate in mechanical engineering, using it only for sedate Sunday afternoon journeys!

The little **"i"** added to the 8000 stands for "intelligence". More than 60 years experience in camera construction, command of modern technology, and cleverly designed electronic controls have been invested in the Dynax. It is more than know-how in precision engineering and the most up-to-date computerised lens design that make the Dynax such a fine camera. It is the experience of literally millions of photographers. Some of the most complex shooting techniques used by photographers were set as tasks to be performed by the Dynax. Some of these experiences have been incorporated in the camera computer; others may be added by the owner through the Creative Expansion Card System that extends the range of camera functions.

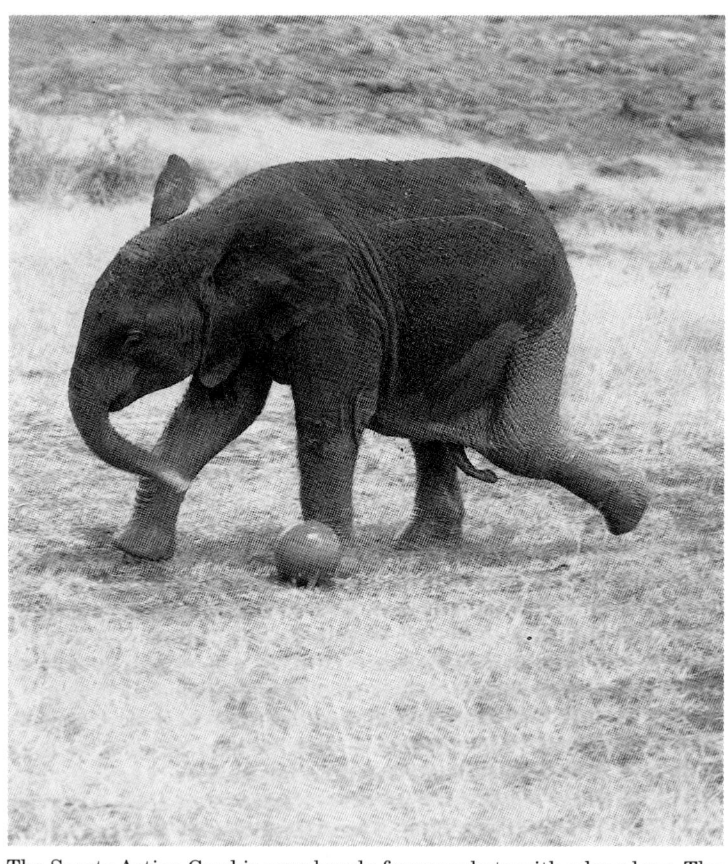

The Sports Action Card is very handy for snapshots with a long lens. The use of this card ensures sufficiently fast shutter speeds for hand-held shots.

Intelligent Autofocus

The sharpness of a picture is one of its most important qualities and that depends on several factors. These are the optical qualities of the lens, the reproduction quality of the film, the size of the aperture, the relative movements of camera and subject, and the speed of the shutter. Then there are atmospheric factors to be considered, such as haze, fog and rain. The most important consideration for the sharpness of the picture, of course, is the distance setting. This task may now be left to the autofocus system of the Dynax 8000i, the most advanced focusing system that has been installed in any SLR camera to date. Its advantages, compared with other systems, are the wider metering area, the automatic function selection between continuous and single focusing, the predictive calculation

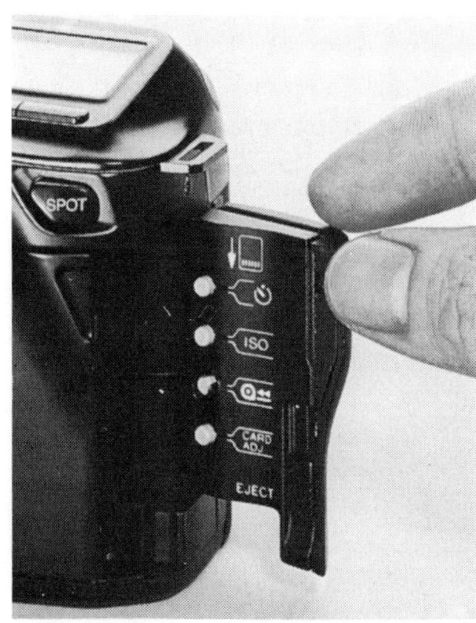

The card door is designed to accommodate not only Creative Expansion Cards for the Minolta Dynax 8000i, but also buttons for functions that are less frequently used such as self-timer, film speed and rewind.

of the speed and direction for moving subjects at continuous focusing, the highly sensitive sensors which are capable of achieving perfect focus even in poor light and the extremely fast focusing speed, enabling up to three frames per second. The integrated AF Illuminator assists the focusing in absolute darkness at distances up to nine meters and is also activated if there is insufficient contrast. The AF Illuminator can in certain circumstances work at a greater range than the specified nine metres. However this does not work with telephoto lenses, which makes a lot of sense anyway, because for focal lengths in excess of 210mm the camera assumes that the subject is much further away than the prescribed nine metres - which is the reason why this function does not work with long lenses.

Large Multi-Sensor Autofocus Area

All previous AF SLR cameras used only a small rectangular AF target area at the centre of the viewfinder for automatic distance setting. In the Dynax 7000i, an

The "Brains" of a Dynax camera:

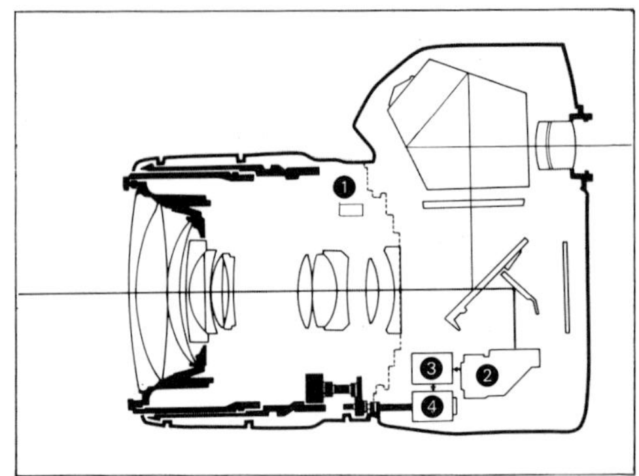

1. ROM-IC
2. AF Module
3. central computer
4. AF motor

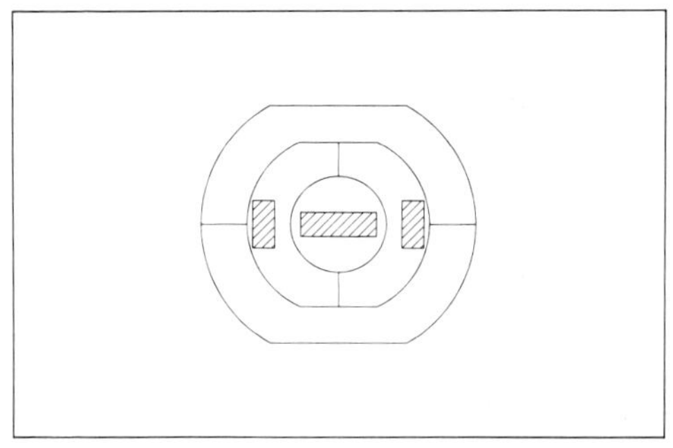

Autofocus-coupled multi-zone exposure metering:
This is how the six metering zones are arranged across the AF focus areas (cross-hatched areas). The weighting of the multi-zone metering distribution is automatically determined by the AF focus area.

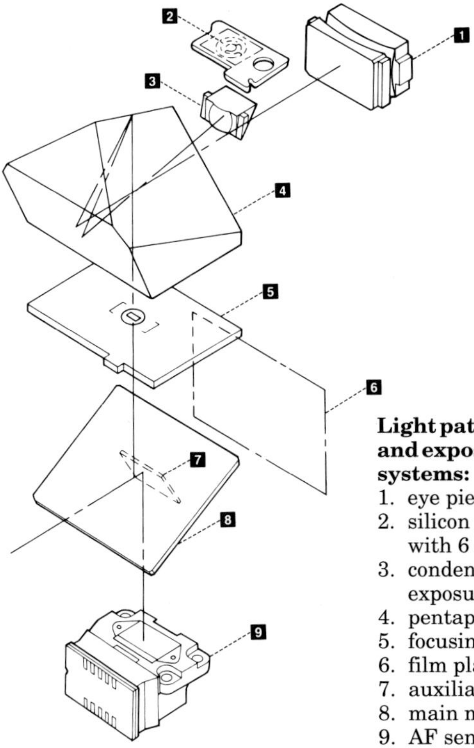

Light path of autofocus and exposure metering systems:

1. eye piece
2. silicon photo diode with 6 segments
3. condenser lens (for exposure metering)
4. pentaprism
5. focusing screen
6. film plane
7. auxiliary mirror
8. main mirror
9. AF sensor module

autofocus system with multi sensors was used for the first time. This system consisted not only of the usual central AF target area with horizontal evaluation, but next to it they put two laterally arranged sensors for vertical assessment of a wider area. The total metering area is now about 12-times the size of conventional AF cameras and this system has been included in the Dynax 8000i.

The chief advantage of this larger focus area is that the main subject is not so difficult to track. One of the problems that arises frequently, is that of a staggered subject, i.e. two objects or persons, standing next to each other, at slightly different distances from the camera. Another problem is poor alignment with the main subject. The wide AF area takes care of these problems. As long as the main subject is anywhere within this area, the Dynax 8000i will ensure that it is in sharp focus. This is particularly noticeable with snapshots; the success rate increases dramatically. It is no longer necessary to take a lot of trouble placing the main subject exactly in the centre of the viewfinder, then realigning for the required frame while keeping the release pressed to store the metered settings. The Dynax 8000i also possesses a focus-hold facility, but this will usually only be necessary for special compositions when you are using the small central AF area.

Slight pressure on the release is sufficient to activate the autofocus of the Dynax 8000i. Point the camera at the main subject, press the release slightly, and the lens moves immediately to the correct focusing position. When sharp focus is obtained, the camera confirms this by the green in-focus signal in the viewfinder. You may now press the release fully to take the picture. In fact the release can only be pressed if the green in-focus signal is showing in the viewfinder.

If the subject is static, i.e. not moving, then the focus setting remains in the memory of the computer as long as the release is kept lightly pressed. This allows the camera to be realigned for more suitable picture framing if required.

The large focus area allows the camera to obtain sharp focus even in situations which are normally considered too difficult for autofocus, for example when the subject is low in contrast or gradation, or lacks definition. The laterally-arranged sensors allow the camera to evaluate features that may not be contained in the central focus area.

Automatic AF Function Selection

With a conventional AF camera the photographer has to set the camera to track a moving subject with autofocus, or assess whether the focus setting for a static subject should be stored and used for the exposure. The brain of the Dynax 8000i has the capability to make this decision entirely unaided. The multi-sensor focusing of the Dynax 8000i recognizes whether the subject moves or not and automatically makes the decision for continuous autofocusing or a single focus setting.

Predictive Autofocus

The camera's computer recognizes that the subject is moving by evaluating the metered data, while at the same time automatically assessing the speed and direction of that movement and whether the subject is

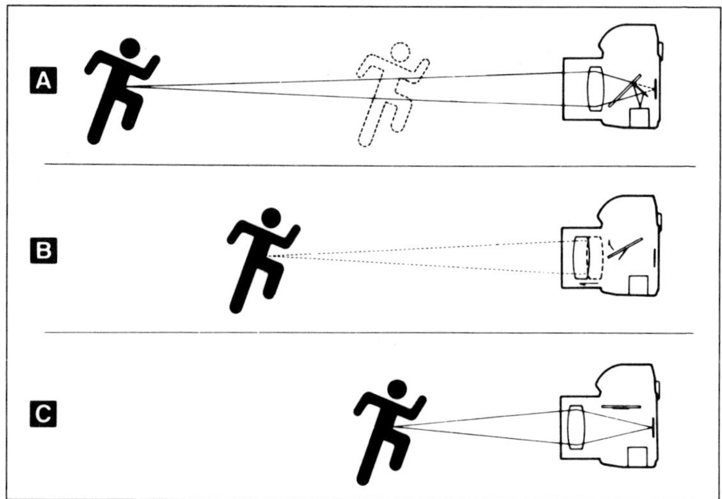

Predictive autofocus: (A) As soon as the release is fully pressed the autofocus control calculates how much further the main subject is going to travel before the shutter blinds will open. (B) the focusing motor continues to adjust the focus setting on the lens while the mirror is raised (C) The autofocus motor stops at the previously-calculated focus setting, just before the shutter is opened.

moving towards or away from the camera. Based on these metering data the AF motor continuously adjusts the distance setting, not only until the release is pressed, but even up to the last moment when the actual exposure is made. This means that the camera keeps on controlling the motor and adjusting the lens, even up to the moment the mirror is raised; it stops only just before the shutter is opened. Conversely, the shutter only opens when the subject in the metering area has been brought into exact focus. The Dynax therefore is the first AF camera to achieve this precise, automatic, focusing of fast-moving subjects.

Up to three frames per second can be taken in the

continuous shooting mode. With the release kept pressed, the camera exposes one frame after the other, always adjusting the exposure and sharpness between each shot. The shutter will only be released if the subject is in sharp focus, and this applies to both single frame and continuous shooting modes. Even if the photographer tries to release the shutter sooner, the camera will prevent it until correct focus has been achieved.

With the focus-hold button automatic focusing can be deactivated at any point; this is useful, for example, if a subject moves parallel to the film plane, or if the subject that you wish to focus on lies outside the AF area. This button can be reprogrammed with the use of the Customized Function Card.

The fast reaction of the Dynax 8000i AF system has been made possible by the use of the wider focus area, and the highly sensitive CCD AF sensors (CCD = Charged Coupled Device = semi conductor chips), more efficient data processing by the camera computer and the integrated high speed autofocus motor.

The appropriate autofocus function is indicated in the viewfinder by LEDs. This display "pulses" i.e. the brackets of the LED move from the inside to the outside, as soon as the camera computer has ascertained that the subject in the focus area is moving. If the movement is too fast for the autofocus then the green LED will not light up. If the contrast is too low, or the prevailing lighting conditions are inadequate, then the red LED will flash. The following displays are possible:

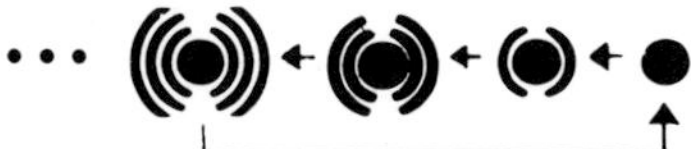

The camera focuses on a

moving subject. The focus is continuously adjusted. The release can be triggered.

... (●) The lens is focused on a static subject. The framing can be changed, focus setting on the lens can be retained. The release can be triggered.

... The subject moves too fast for automatic focusing. The release cannot be triggered.

... Automatic focusing is not possible because of too low contrast, too little light, or because the subject is too close. The release is locked. Change to manual focusing.

Centre Autofocus Area

The large autofocus area is not ideal for all situations. For example, if you are taking a close-up and wish to focus precisely on a certain detail within the frame, or if you wish to pick out a certain person within a crowd.

In such situations a smaller focus area would produce better results. For this reason the Dynax 8000i provides a choice between a large and a small, conventional focus area. Press the function-selector key until the pointer is beneath the focus-area indicator in the LCD panel. Now press the **FUNC** button and push the setting control to select the required focus area. A centre focus indicator also appears in the viewfinder display.

Resetting to the large metering field can be done by again using the **FUNC** button and setting control. It can also be reset by pressing the program reset button **P.** However, this will reset other functions to

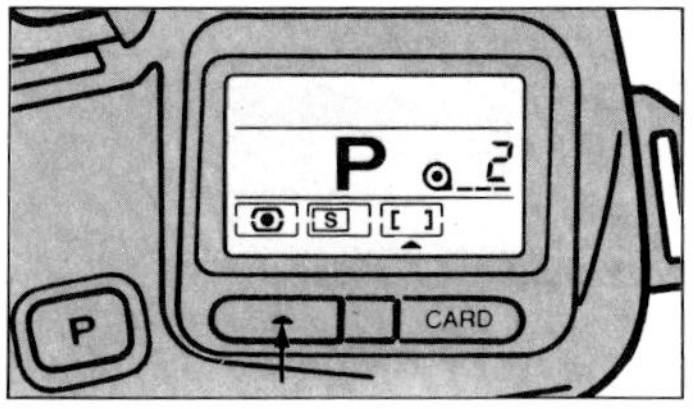

This is how the AF target field is selected:
1. Press the function-selector key until the pointer is beneth the focus area indicator in the LCD panel.

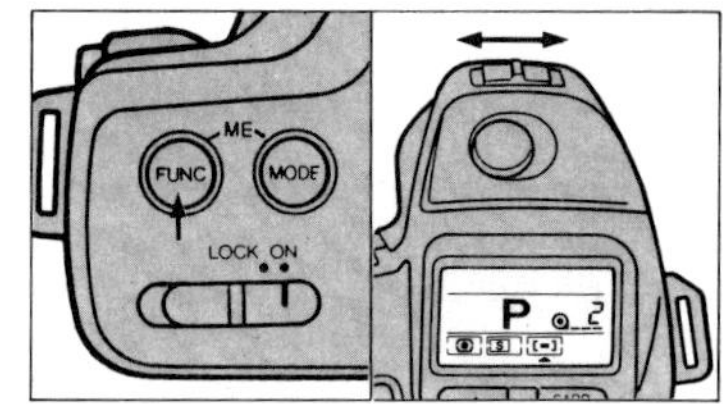

2. Press the **FUNC** button and select either the centre or the wide focus area by pushing the setting control to the right or left. The selected focus area will be displayed in the LCD panel and in the viewfinder.

program mode, autofocus and single frame shooting and any exposure compensations to zero.

Manual Focusing

Occasionally, manual focus is needed for exceptional circumstances. For example, for subjects with poor contrast; i.e. small, uniformly-lit areas, such as a clear sky or a white wall, or if you are dealing with structures with little or no contrast. In this case slide down the focus mode switch which is next to the lens bayonet-mount. Now you can adjust the focus manually by turning the distance setting ring on the lens. Check the focus visually on the focusing screen and use the green LED in-focus signal to assist you. This LED is activated as soon as the release is pressed and lights up if the camera senses the correct focus setting.

Selection of manual focusing is indicated in the LCD panel by M.FOCUS. In this mode the Dynax 8000i may be released at any time, even if exact focus has not been

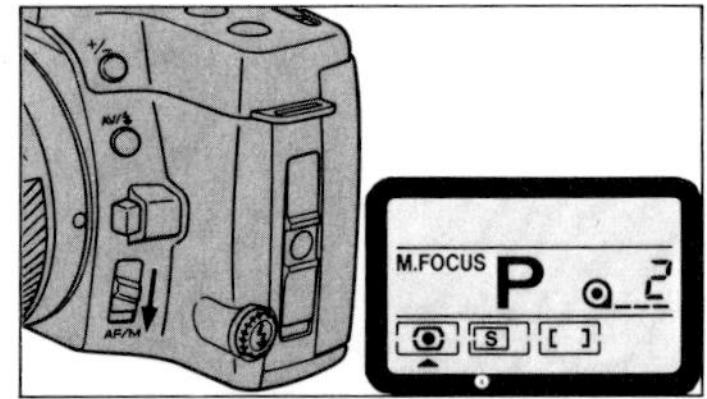

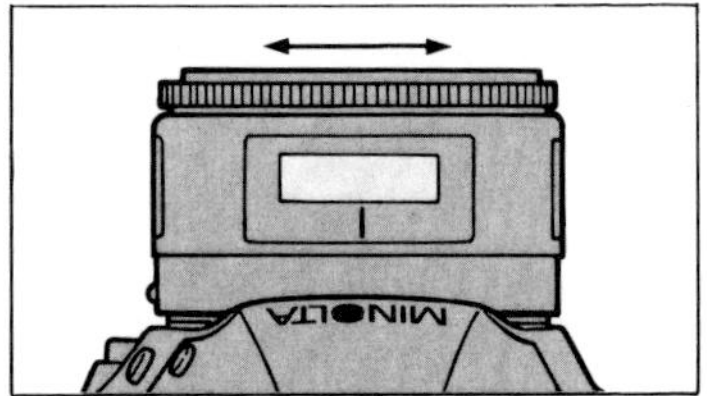

Use the Focus-mode switch to select manual focus, **M.FOCUS** will appear in the LCD panel (left), the lens can now be focused manually (right)

achieved. Manual focus may be cancelled by sliding down the focus mode switch again.

Viewfinder Displays for Manual Focus Setting

Lens is focused.

Focus cannot be confirmed and has to be assessed by the photographer on the focusing screen.

Exposure Metering

Combination of Multi-sensor Autofocus and Multi-Field Metering

The Dynax 7000i was the first SLR camera to incorporate a functional linking of autofocus and exposure metering. In retrospect this innovation appears to be the most logical facility that every camera should have as the exposure should be correct for the main subject on which the camera is focused. This was made possible by the combination of multi-sensor autofocus on the one hand and the six-segment exposure metering on the other. This means that the computer in the Dynax 8000i controls the sensitivity distribution for exposure metering depending on the subject distance and position.

Variable Sensitivity of Metering Segments

The metering of the subject is performed by a six-segment silicon photo diode in the pentaprism of the camera. Each individual segment of the photo diode has variable light sensitivity, allowing measurement of various brightness distributions. The metering system is thus capable of taking an average reading, a nulti-pattern reading, or a spot reading.

By comparing the brightness of the main subject and the background, the camera can ascertain whether the subject is uniformly lit. It is capable of automatically assessing whether the subject is backlit or if it is spotlit.

The calculation of the brightness differences between main subject and its surrounding area forms the basis for the automatic contrast compensation in the exposure metering. The camera computer performs all these calculations in real time, i.e. it automatically processes all autofocus and light data to ensure, at all times, optimum metering distribution. The computer performs all these tasks in microseconds in order to be able to control and initiate the camera functions. It performs the exposure calculations as follows. After ascertaining the sharpness, the computer determines what position the focused main subject occupies in the frame. The computer then calculates the reproduction ratio from the subject distance and the focal length data that have been transferred by the ROM-IC (Read Only Memory Integrated Circuit). The sensitivity distribution of the multi-zone exposure metering is then determined from the position of the main subject in the frame. As the system works without delay, the sensitivity distribution immediately follows any changes in the position of the subject or its distance to

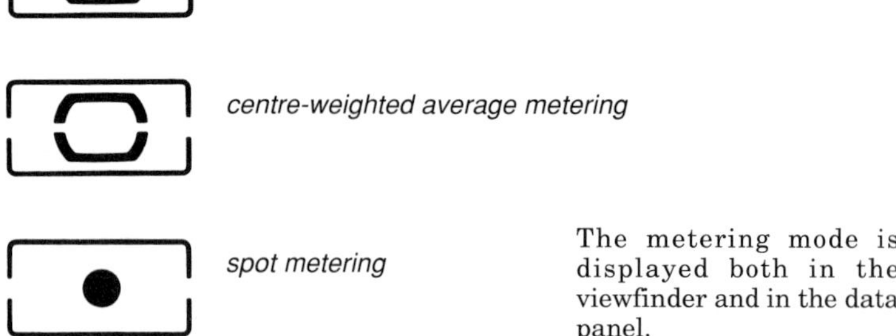

The metering mode is displayed both in the viewfinder and in the data panel.

the lens. Once taken, the exposure readings and focus settings are stored by pressing the release half-way down and holding it there. The photographer can use this facility to store the data and realign the camera for the required framing and place the main subject in any position within that frame.

Spot Metering

For special tasks it may be advantageous to meter important subject parts precisely. For this purpose the Dynax 8000i has a central spot metering facility in addition to multi-pattern and centre weighted average metering. To switch to spot metering press the **SPOT** button at the rear of the camera. Contrary to centre weighted average metering and multi-pattern metering, spot metering is activated only as long as the **SPOT** button is pressed. As soon as it is released the camera will again measure in the mode that has been previously selected. The area for spot metering is defined by the small circle at the centre of the focusing screen. This represents about 2.3% of the picture area.

To use spot metering, first point the camera at the subject as usual and focus. It does not matter whether this is done manually or by autofocus. Then ensure

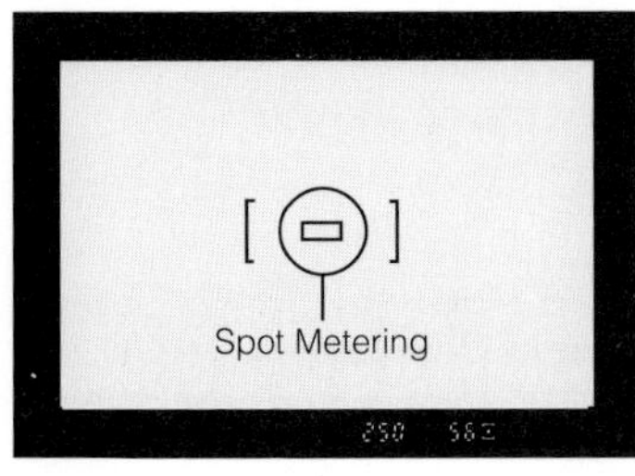

This is how spot metering is used:
1. Point camera at main subject and focus lens.
2. Cover the important subject detail with the spot metering circle at the centre of the focusing screen and press and hold the **SPOT** button.

that the subject area that has to be optimally exposed is fully covered by the spot metering circle at the centre of the focusing screen and press and hold the **SPOT** button. The metered value is retained for as long as the **SPOT** button is kept pressed. If you are shooting in one of the auto exposure modes this button must be kept pressed until the shutter is released. If you are shooting in manual exposure mode, remember the metering values and set them manually.

The **SPOT** button may also be used to obtain longer flash synchronization speeds when using the Dynax 8000i with a Minolta program flash gun. This subject is covered in the chapter Minolta Program Flash Guns.

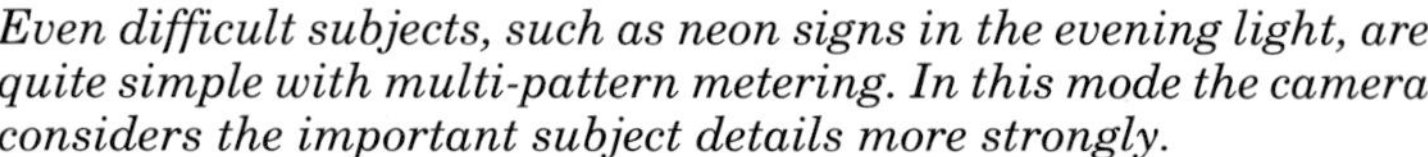

Even difficult subjects, such as neon signs in the evening light, are quite simple with multi-pattern metering. In this mode the camera considers the important subject details more strongly. ⇨

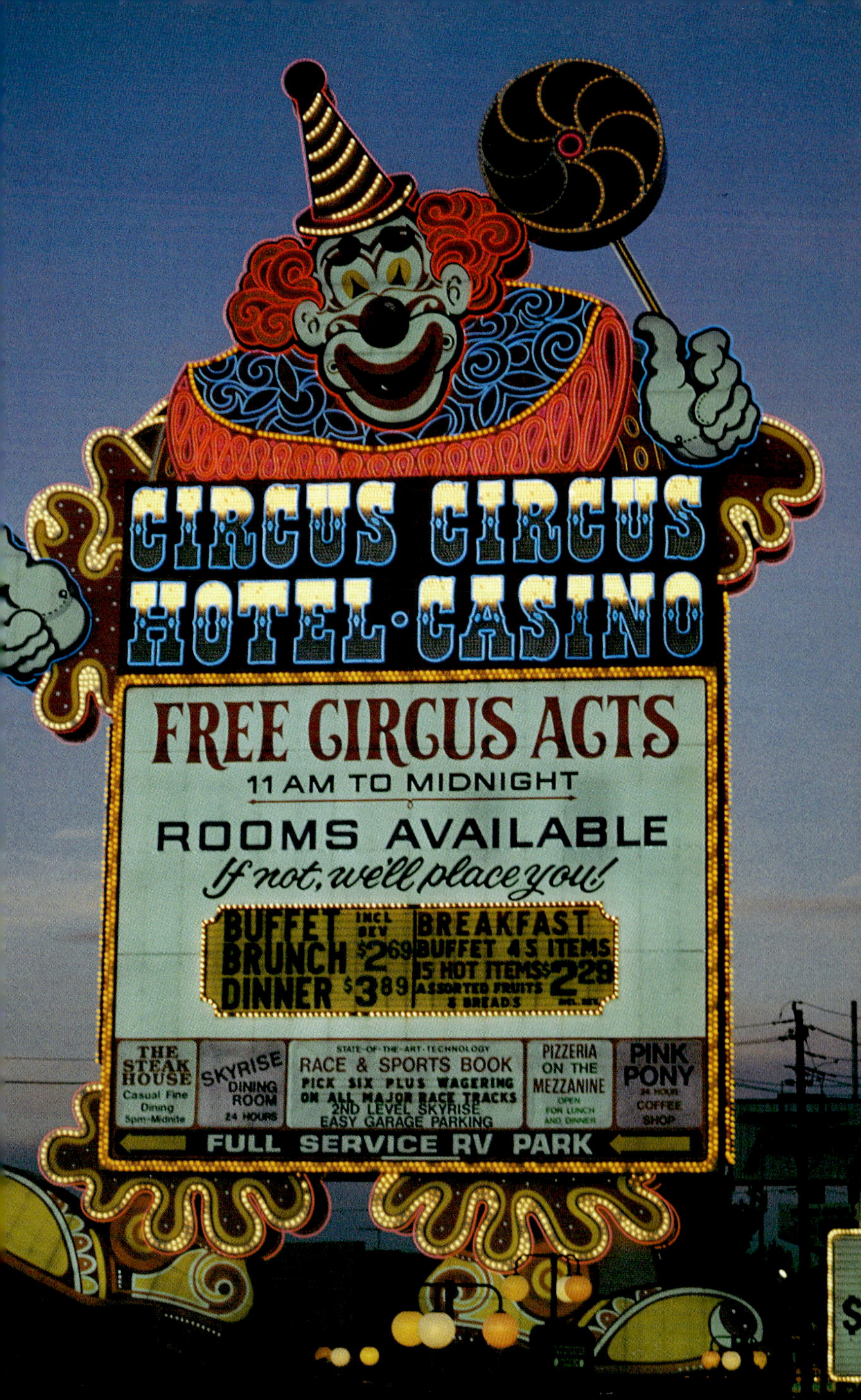

CIRCUS CIRCUS
HOTEL·CASINO
FREE CIRCUS ACTS
11 AM TO MIDNIGHT
ROOMS AVAILABLE
If not, we'll place you!
BUFFET BRUNCH INCL BEV $2.69
DINNER $3.89
BREAKFAST BUFFET 45 ITEMS
15 HOT ITEMS $2.28
ASSORTED FRUITS & BREADS
THE STEAK HOUSE
Casual Fine Dining
SKYRISE DINING ROOM
24 HOURS
STATE-OF-THE-ART-TECHNOLOGY
RACE & SPORTS BOOK
PICK SIX PLUS WAGERING
ON ALL MAJOR RACE TRACKS
2ND LEVEL SKYRISE
EASY GARAGE PARKING
PIZZERIA ON THE MEZZANINE
PINK PONY
COFFEE SHOP
FULL SERVICE RV PARK

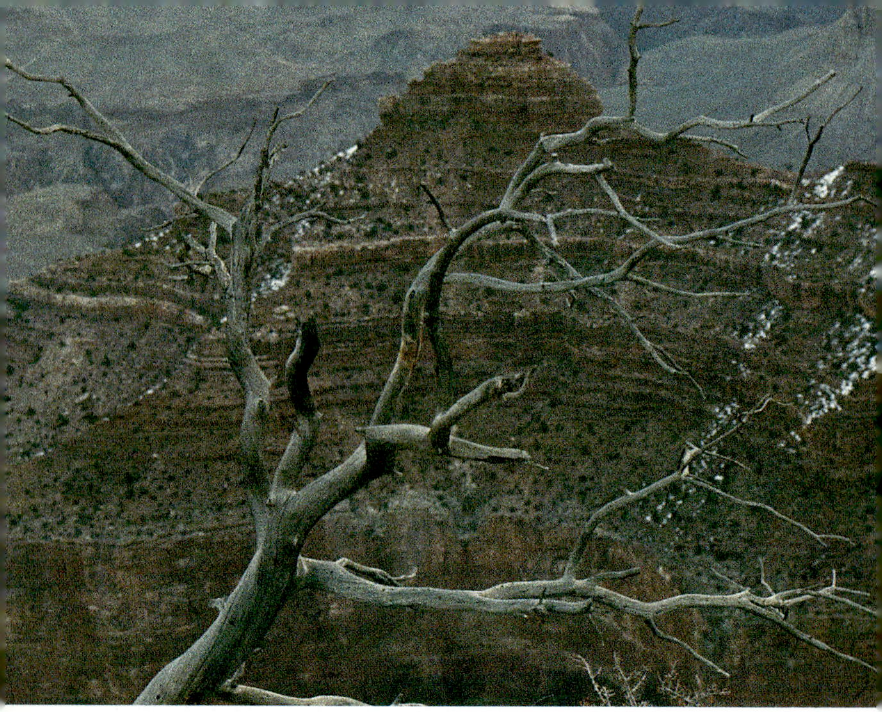

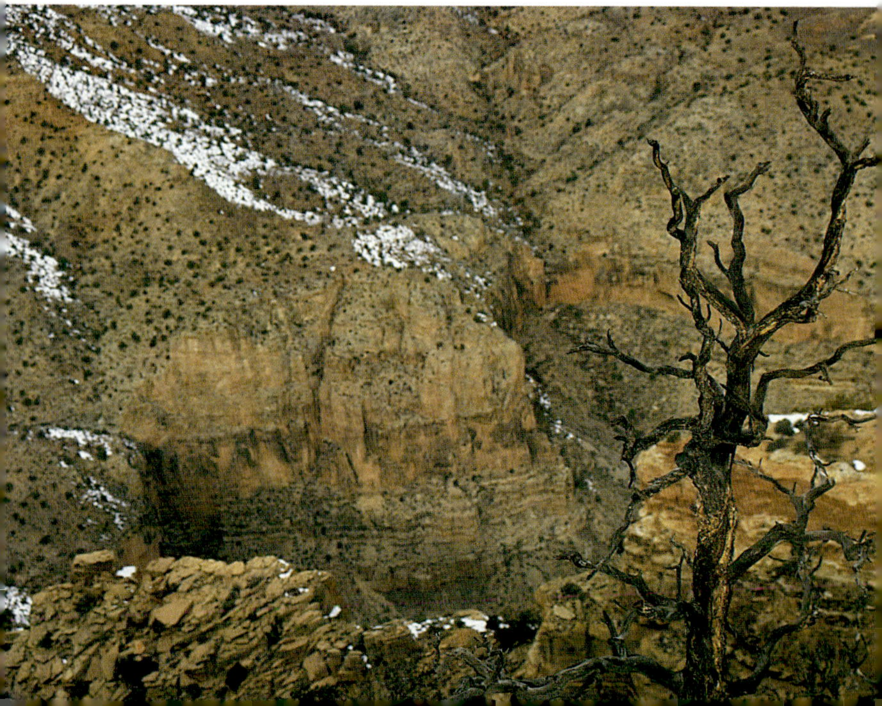

Exposure Control

Automatic Multi Program Selection

Apart from the release, the program reset button, **P**, is the most important button on the Dynax 8000i. This button resets all camera functions to fully automatic mode. Focus and exposure are automatically selected without the photographer's intervention. All previously selected settings and special functions are cancelled when this button is pressed.

The fully automatic mode with multi program control is the most convenient shooting mode of the Dynax 8000i. This mode is indicated by a large **P** in the LCD panel. In this shooting mode the Dynax 8000i selects the most suitable combination of shutter speed and aperture to obtain correct exposure. In doing so, it not only considers the prevailing lighting conditions, but also the focal length of the attached lens, and will endeavour to select a suitable shutter speed for hand-held shots. If a zoom lens is attached, the camera can even ascertain the selected zoom settings and allows for changing focal length settings in its calculations. If you move the ring on a zoom you can observe how the camera adjusts this. The information about which focal length lens or zoom setting is used is supplied by

---

Structures and strong lines are the key to these striking compositions. The use of a zoom lens – in this case the Minolta AF 70-210mm, f/3.5-4.5, allowed the choice of the most suitable framing without having to change the shooting position.

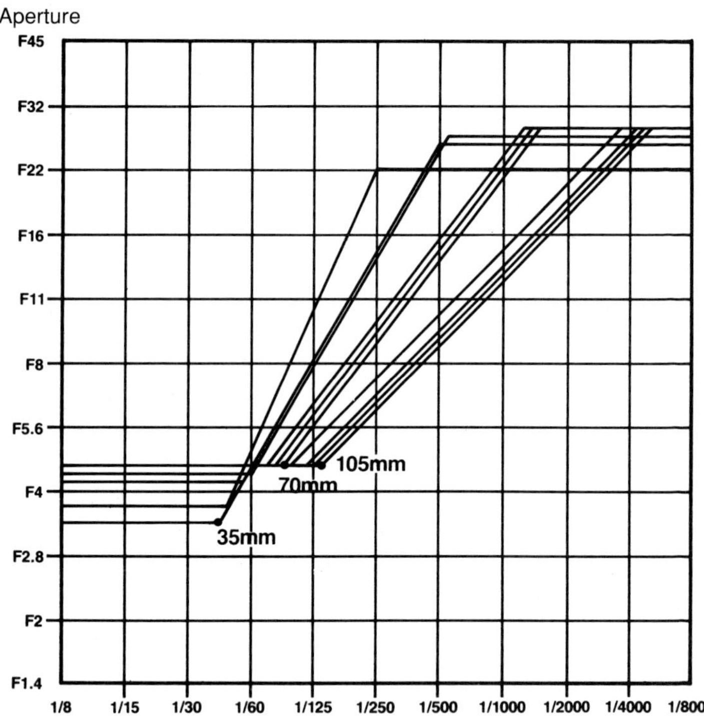

The automatic multi-program selection of the Minolta Dynax 8000i controls the exposure settings depending on the focal length of the attached lens. This example shows the curves for the Minolta AF 35-105mm, f/3.5-4.5 zoom.

the ROM-Integrated Circuit in the Minolta AF lens. This supplies the camera computer with all the necessary lens information and is absolutely essential for automatic program selection. This is also the reason why some other manufacturers, who do not buy their chips from Minolta, find it difficult to provide lenses for the Minolta Dynax 8000i. If the camera is unable to read the ROM of another manufacturer's lens, or if it is not able to read it properly, then the display in the viewfinder or the LCD panel is incomplete or not given at all. In extreme cases it is even possible that such a

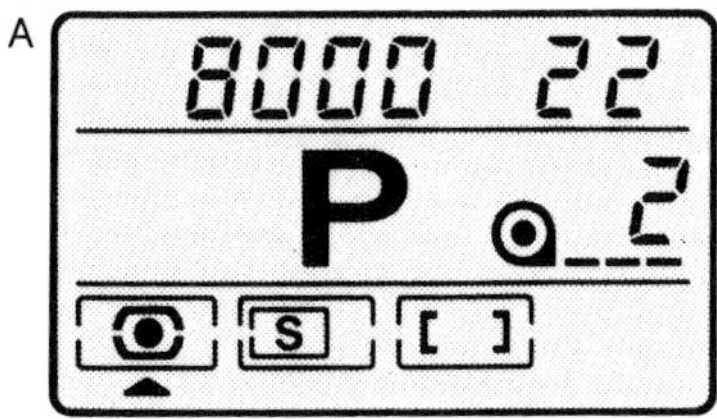

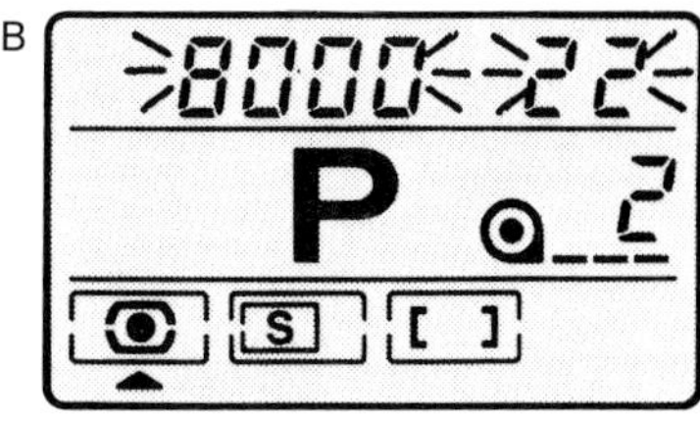

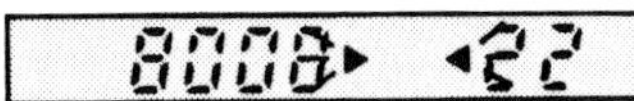

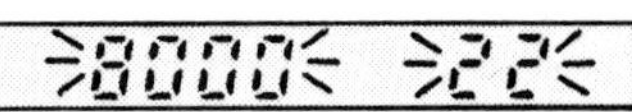

Whenever the available light is insufficient for a correct exposure, the metering indicators in the viewfinder (A) flash. If the required exposure value lies outside the available setting range of the camera, then **8000** and the smallest available aperture value flash in the viewfinder and the data panel (B). If the light is too low it is best to use a Minilta Program flashgun, in too bright light the use of a neutral density filter should remedy the situation.

lens may damage the electronics of the Dynax 8000i. It is therefore important to ensure that a non-Minolta lens used with the Dynax 8000i, has been manufactured under licence.

The choice of the exposure program is determined by the focal length of the lens. The automatic program selection gives preference to faster shutter speeds to ensure that hand-held shots are without camera shake. The correct shutter speeds correspond to the rule which says that the shutter speed should not be slower than that fraction of a second represented by the reciprocal of the focal length of the lens.

For example, if you are using a 200mm lens this would be 1/200 sec, so the shutter speed should not be any slower than 1/250 sec; for a 135mm lens the shutter speed would be 1/125 sec.

There are other cameras that are capable of adjusting their exposure program for the focal length of the attached lens. However, no other camera at present on the market is capable of such a variety of automatically-controlled exposure programs. When the camera is set to program mode the multi-pattern metering, coupled with the AF metering system, is always selected.

Program Shift

The more advanced photographer will not always be satisfied with the camera's decision regarding the most suitable shutter speed for hand-held shots. He may use a tripod to support his camera with a long lens, or he may want to catch a fast moving subject with a wide-angle lens. The Dynax 8000i has a very useful facility for such cases - the program shift.

In this mode it is possible temporarily to select different shutter speed/aperture combinations to those selected by the camera, without having to change over to shutter speed priority or aperture priority mode, and without having to worry about incorrect exposure settings. The exposure value itself is not changed when

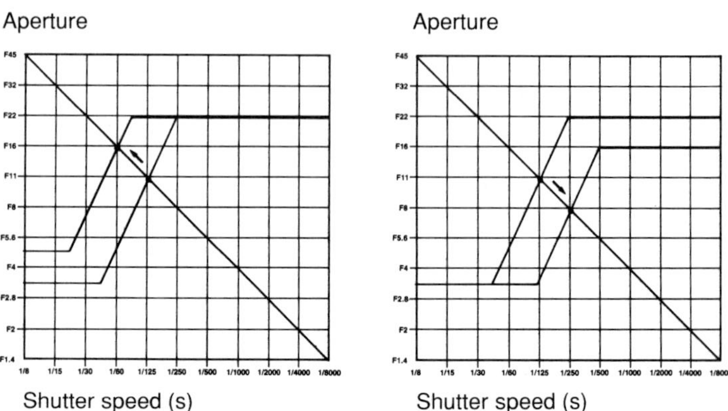

If the shutter speed/aperture combination suggested by the camera does not fit in with the creative intentions of the photographer, then they can be adjusted at any time by using the program shift facility, this will not affect the exposure value which is kept constant.

program shift is in operation, as this mode will only allow aperture/shutter speed combinations which will produce correct exposure.

At this point it may be convenient to include a little theory on exposure. A photograph is created by the light falling through the lens onto the film. In order to create a suitable image on the film only a certain amount of light is allowed to expose the film. Not too much and not too little. Too much light leads to overexposure, too little light to underexposure. The amount of light that is allowed to pass through the lens onto the film is controlled by two parameters - shutter speed and aperture. The shutter speed determines how long the light is allowed to affect the film, the aperture opening determines how much light is allowed through at any one time. The process may be compared with a tap; the amount of water depends on how wide you open the tap and how long you leave it open. A large aperture opening allows a lot of light through, a small one allows only a little light through. It is therefore possible to bring the same amount of light onto the film by using a small aperture and keeping the shutter open for a long time or the other way round by opening the aperture wide and making the shutter speed very fast. The numbers identifying the apertures are a little confusing: Large numbers, i.e. 11 16 22 and larger identify small apertures, small numbers such as 1.4 2.8 and 4 identify large apertures.

The user of a Dynax 8000i can select faster shutter speeds by activating the setting control to avoid movement blur in action photographs. The camera will automatically open up the aperture to compensate for the faster shutter speed to keep the correct exposure level. On the other hand, if the shutter speed is decreased then the camera will automatically stop down the aperture to compensate for the slower shutter speed.

The program shift facility makes the shutter speed priority and aperture priority modes practically superfluous as well as being very convenient to use. After taking the measurement, the setting control is used to shift the automatically selected combination. Pushing it to the left will decrease the shutter speed and stop down the aperture; pushing it to the right opens up the aperture and increases the shutter speed. The changes are performed in half stops.

The program shift is retained for about five seconds after taking the finger off the release. The camera then automatically changes back to normal program mode. If the shift needs to be retained longer than five seconds, then the release has to be kept lightly pressed. When shooting with zoom lenses the program shift should be applied after the focal length has been selected, because the programmed values are constantly changing with the changing focal length.

Practical Tips

Fast shutter speeds are necessary to freeze fast movements. On the other hand it is possible to produce very impressive images with slower shutter speeds by following the subject; a technique called panning.

Aperture and shutter speed are not only a means to control the amount of exposure, they are also an important creative tool. The size of the aperture determines the depth in front of and behind the focused subject which is also reproduced in acceptably sharp focus. For large apertures this is rather small. For small apertures this spatial depth increases. This is useful, for example, in portrait photography, where the background can be made to look unobtrusive by depicting it as out of focus. In landscape photography, on the other hand, a small aperture will bring the entire subject, from close-up to infinity, into acceptably sharp focus.

Aperture Priority Mode

If the depth of field is important, then it would be best to set the Dynax 8000i to aperture priority mode. In this mode the aperture is set by the photographer and the camera's exposure control will select the appropriate shutter speed for that aperture value. To select this mode, press the **MODE** button and push the setting control in either direction until A appears in the LCD panel. A small pointer on the top line of the data panel will now point at the aperture value to indicate that this may be changed manually by the setting control.

If you are looking for an aperture ring on your AF lens, then you will be looking in vain. The aperture selection is performed via the camera computer, similar to the system used by all other Minolta autofocus SLR cameras. To select the required aperture value in aperture priority mode you simply push the setting control to the right for larger apertures and to the left for smaller ones. Each time the control is moved one way or the other the aperture is adjusted in half stops.

Depending on your photographic intent, you may now select a large aperture to set the main subject

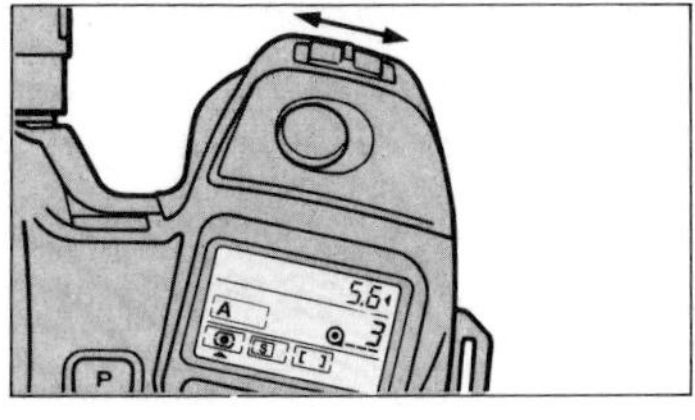

Preselection of aperture value: In A mode, push the setting control to increase or decrease the displayed value; this is usually done to determine the depth of field. The camera will automatically select a suitable shutter speed.

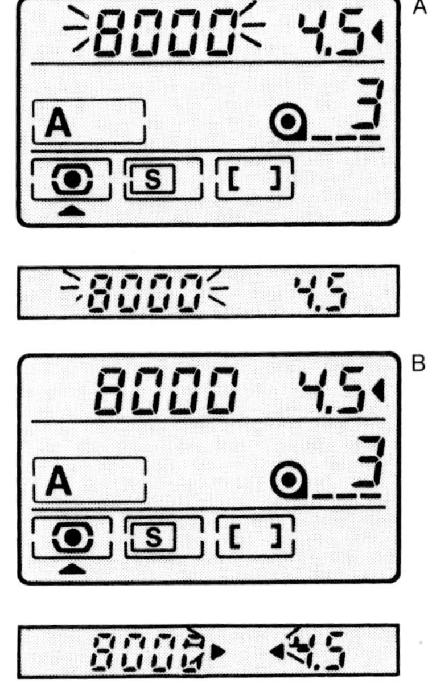

If the selected shutter speed lies outside the available range the shutter speed display flashes in the data panel (A). If **8000** flashes, select a small enough aperture to stop the shutter speed display flashing. If **30** flashes, then a larger aperature has to be selected until the display stops flashing. If both the viewfinder metering indicators flash, then it is either too bright or too dark to achieve a correct exposure level.

against a hazy, blurred background, or choose a small aperture to bring everything to sharp focus.

If the chosen aperture necessitates a shutter speed that lies outside the range of the Dynax 8000i, then the shutter speed display will flash. If the "8000" flashes, then this means that a smaller aperture has to be chosen to prevent overexposure. Simply use the setting control to stop down the aperture, half a stop at a time, until the shutter speed display stops flashing. If "30" - the slowest automatically-controllable shutter speed - flashes, then the aperture needs to be opened up to prevent underexposure. Again, move the setting control until the shutter speed display stops flashing. If the light is too strong or too dim and the exposure reading indicates that no satisfactory settings may be obtained, then the two triangular exposure signals will

A

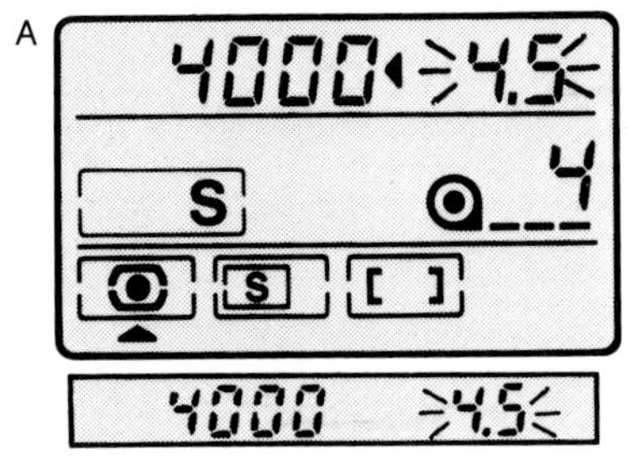

B

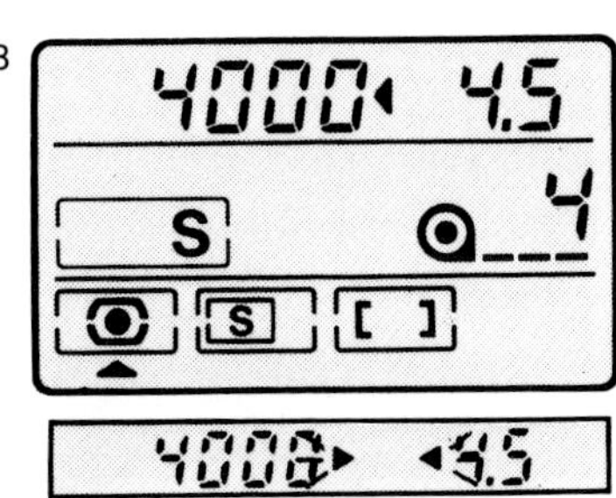

If the smallest aperture value flashes in the data panel, select a fast enough shutter speed to stop it flashing. If the largest aperture value blinks, a slower shutter speed has to be selected (A). If both metering indicators in the viewfinder flashes, then it is either too bright or too dark to achieve a correct exposure level (B). If the light is too dim, you could use a Minolta Program flash.
In **S** mode do not use **bulb** setting (long exposure). This setting may be used only in manual mode.

flash in the viewfinder.stops, the shutter speed, on the other hand, only in full stops. However, it is possible to reprogram the Dynax 8000i with the Customized Function card to enable the shutter speed to be changed in half stops.

Shutter Speed Priority Mode

The use of shutter speed priority mode is particularly useful when taking fast-moving subjects such as racing cars, and also for sports and action photography,

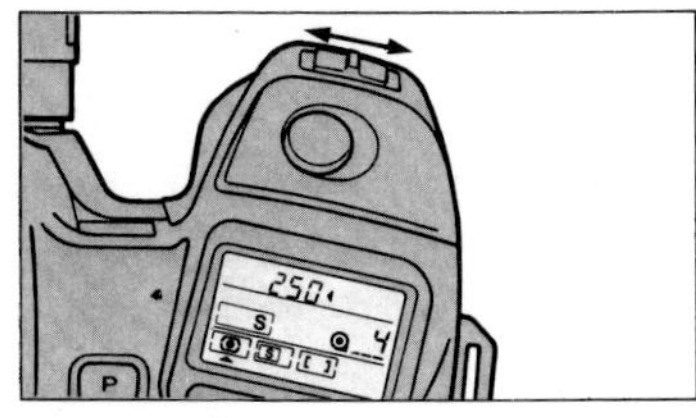

Preselection of shutter speed: In **S** mode, push the setting control to the left to select slower shutter speeds, to the right for faster ones. The value always changes by one f/stop.

etc. In this shooting mode a particular shutter speed may be manually preselected and the camera will choose the appropriate aperture value to suit the lighting conditions. If you wish to present a fast-moving racing car sharply in the picture, you can preselect one of the fast shutter speeds, for example 1/2000 or 1/4000 sec, even 1/8000 sec if the conditions are really bright. For speed-blurred effects with panning you will need slower shutter speeds. The automatically controlled shutter speed of the Dynax 8000i ranges from an impressive 1/8000 down to 30 sec. The highly efficient motor with sophisticated brake mechanism ensures stable operating conditions across the whole shutter speed range.

To select shutter speed priority mode, press the **MODE** button and push the setting control in either direction until **S** is displayed in the middle line of the LCD panel. Now a small arrow will point to the shutter speed display to indicate that the shutter speed may be changed manually.

Pushing the setting control to the right selects faster shutter speeds and pushing it to the left chooses slower speeds. The shutter speed is stepped through in full stops. It is possible to reprogram the camera function to change the shutter speed in half stop intervals by using the Customized Function card.

If the aperture value flashes, this means that the available apertures of the attached lens are insufficient to allow correct exposure settings for the preselected shutter speed. If the minimum aperture (largest f/number) of the attached lens blinks, then the shutter speed has to be increased. If the maximum aperture (smallest f/number) flashes then the shutter speed has to be reduced. If the subject is too dark or too light to obtain satisfactory exposure settings, then the two indicators for the exposure metering in the viewfinder will flash.

Manual Setting of Shutter Speed and Aperture

There are situations when the photographer may wish to create special effects: previously determined under- or overexposure, where targeted measurements of particular subject details may produce a singularly effective image. Here too the Dynax 8000i allows the photographer to bring his creative skill into effect. For special circumstances or photographic intent the Dynax 8000i can be manually controlled. In this mode too, the photographer is fully informed of all important data by the LCD panel and viewfinder display. He will be informed whether his chosen settings of aperture/shutter speed combination will run the risk of under- or overexposure, or if they agree with the camera's calculated values.

To change to manual mode, press the **MODE** button and push the setting control until **M** is displayed in the middle line of the LCD panel. The small arrows next to shutter speed and aperture value indicate that both of these may now be adjusted manually.

A slight pressure on the release will now activate the autofocus and exposure metering systems. The metering system will be activated as long as the release is kept pressed. The selected values for aperture and shutter speed appear in the LCD panel and two small triangles between the shutter speed and aperture value in the viewfinder display. These indicate whether the manually-selected values correspond to the cam-

Preselection of shutter speed: In **M** mode, push the setting control to the right for faster shutter speeds, to the left for slower ones. The value always changes in full f/stops.

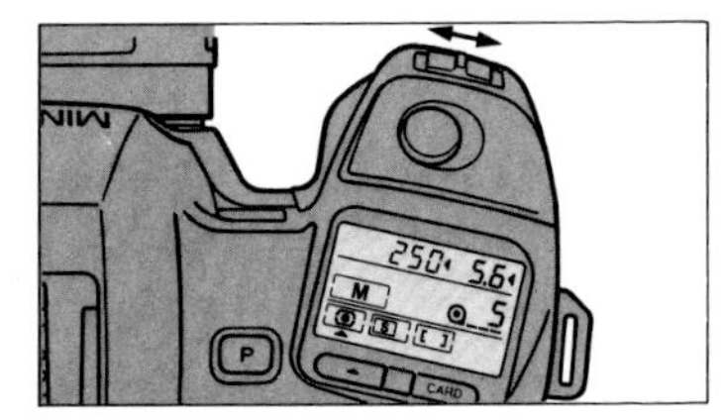

Preselection of aperture: In **M** mode, push and hold the aperture button while moving the setting control to the right to obtain larger apertures (smaller f/numbers), and to the left for smaller apertures (larger f/numbers). The aperture display increased or decreased in half stops.

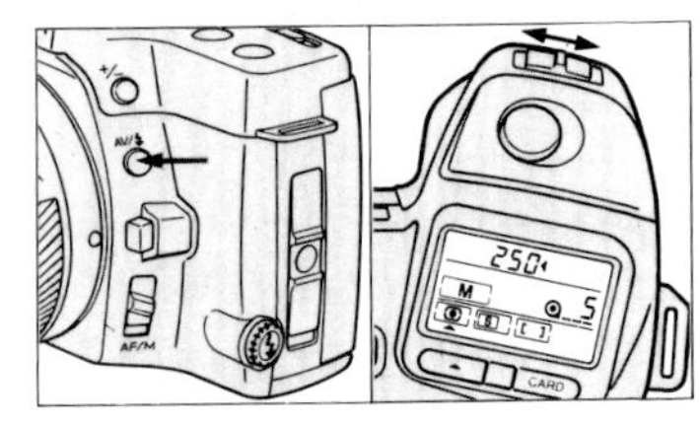

Indicators for exposure metering: If both viewfinder indicators illuminate the exposure is correct. If the left one lights up together with the + sign the selected values would cause overexposure. Warning of underexposure is given by the right indicator and the – symbol illuminating. If the range is exceeded both indicators flash.

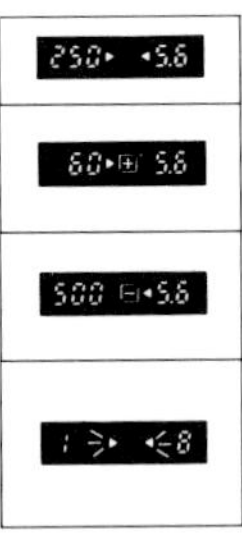

era's exposure calculations. Both of these triangles light up if the selected settings correspond to a correct exposure. For overexposure, the left triangle lights up, together with a plus sign in a square. The triangle points in the direction which the setting control has to be pushed to correct the settings. In the case of overexposure the setting control has to be pushed to the right to correct the setting. For underexposure the display is similar, only now there is a minus sign in the square, and the triangle pointing to the left is lit. It does not matter whether the aperture value or the shutter speed is changed. To change the shutter speed only the setting control is needed, but to change the aperture the aperture-setting button situated on the left of the lens, marked **AV**/flash symbol, has to be kept pressed as well as using the setting control.

If both pointers flash, the camera's setting range is exceeded. The light level is beyond the meter's range and no correct exposure can be obtained.

In manual mode the aperture values may be changed in intervals of half stops, the shutter speed, on the other hand, only in full stops. However, it is possible to reprogram the Dynax 8000i with the Customized Function card to enable the shutter speed to be changed in half stops.

It is recommended that the centre-weighted average or spot metering facility be used in manual mode, as this allows you to expose the main subject precisely.

Manual Exposure Compensation

To a certain degree correct exposure is a matter of interpretation but it also depends on the film material used. If you are using a slide film it is generally considered advantageous to underexpose by half a stop, as this makes the projected images appear stronger and the colours richer. For colour prints slight overexposure often improves the quality. If you wish to make

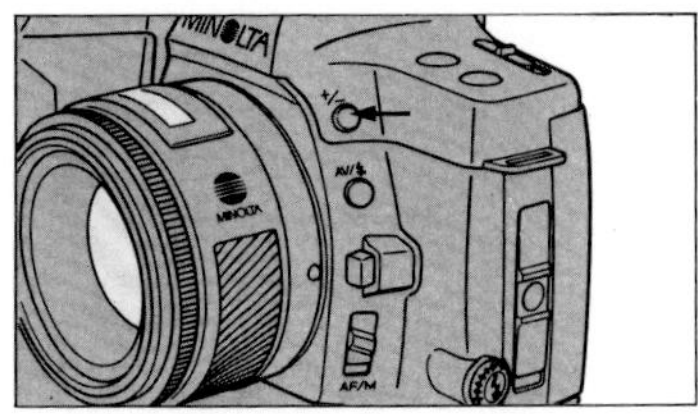

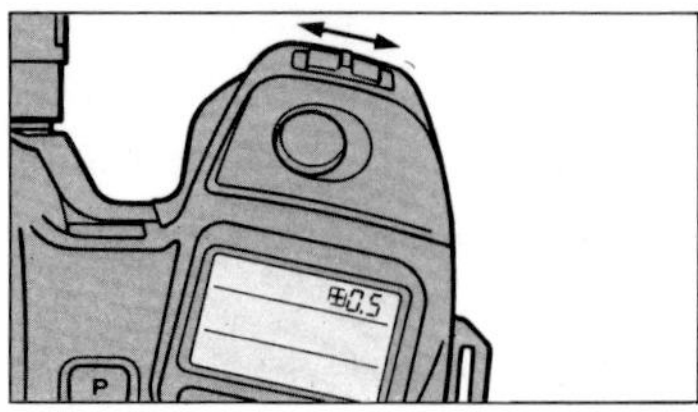

If the exposure adjustment button, marked +/–, is pressed, the exposure can be compensated in the range of +/– 4 EV in half-stop intervals by using the setting control.

such exposure compensations it is no problem with the Dynax 8000i; apart from the override of the automatic film speed setting there is also a manual exposure compensation facility. To use this simply press and hold the exposure-adjustment button, marked "+/-", next to the pentaprism and enter the required compensation by the setting control. Pushing the setting control to the left reduces the exposure compensation, pushing the control to the right increases it. Compensations of up to +/- four aperture stops in half stop increments can be selected in this way. If an exposure compensation is selected, then this is indicated in the viewfinder and the LCD panel by the + or - symbol. The actual amount of compensation can be read off the LCD panel by pressing the exposure adjustment button again.

Any selected exposure compensation is cancelled by pressing the **P** button which sets the camera back to fully automatic mode. Therefore, if you wish to retain an exposure compensation when changing the exposure program from shutter speed priority mode, aperture priority mode, or manual mode back to fully automatic program mode, you have to use the **MODE** button and the setting control.

Long Exposure Times

The Dynax 8000i is ideally suited for long exposures. However, for times in excess of 30 sec you will have to use a hand-held exposure meter to ascertain the correct exposure.

Long exposure times will be necessary, for example, to capture a fireworks display, or night shots of illuminated buildings. The **bulb** setting is provided for this purpose. First set the camera to manual mode, then push and hold the setting control to the left until **bulb** appears in the LCD panel. The aperture is set by pressing the aperture-setting button simultaneously with pushing the setting control.

The **bulb** setting will be used mainly in low light conditions. The long exposure times mean you will have to support the camera on a tripod to avoid camera shake. Take care not to over-tighten the tripod screw as this may damage the camera body. The tripod screw must not be any longer than 5mm.

In the **bulb** setting the shutter remains open as long as the release is kept pressed. To avoid camera shake whilst holding down the release a remote release cable is recommended, either the RC-1000S (50cm long) or the RC-1000L (5m long), which are available as accessories. They have a lockable release so you need not keep your finger on the button all the time the shutter is open. The cable connects to a terminal, concealed by a small cover, below the card door.

Long exposures require more energy than other shooting modes causing a weak battery to become completely exhausted. In this case the camera will not transport the film after the exposure has been made and you will have to change the battery.

Self-timer

The electronic self-timer in modern cameras is not only for the photographer who wants to set himself in the picture. A very useful application is to use it instead of a remote release cable for long exposures. The self-timer of the Dynax 8000i delays the release of the shutter by 10 sec.

This facility is not used very often and so the button is concealed in the card door and marked by the international symbol of a clock face. If this button is pressed, the self-timer symbol is displayed in the LCD panel. Now you can choose the frame and focus on the subject. The focus is best set by changing over to manual focusing. Before the self-timer is pressed it is important to place the cover over the eyepiece to avoid incorrect exposures because of light entering through it. As soon as the sequence has started, the red light at the front of the camera starts flashing at the rate of twice a second, stopping the moment the exposure is made. The self-timer is automatically cancelled after each exposure. If you wish to stop the self-timer sequence once it has begun, either press the program reset button **P**, which will cancel all other functions as well, or set the main switch to **LOCK.** If the count-down has not commenced, the self-timer mode can be cancelled by pressing the self-timer button again.

Film Speed Setting

Aperture and shutter speed both control the amount of light that is allowed to expose the film. How much light the film needs for correct exposure is described in terms of film speed. The standard for this used to be defined in either the DIN or the ASA scale. Today we use the ISO standard. A film that used to be defined as 21 DIN or 100 ASA is now called ISO 100/21°. Doubling the ASA value means the film speed is twice that of the previous value, and this in turn corresponds to one aperture stop. The logarithmic number increases by three for twice the film speed. This is also expressed in the ISO notation. For example, an ISO 200/24° film is twice as fast as an ISO 100/21° film.

Most modern cameras, including the Dynax 8000i, are capable of reading the film speed coding, which was introduced by Kodak, from the bar code on the film cassette. The camera reads the chessboard-like pattern on the cassette via 19 contacts in the film chamber, and passes this information to the exposure metering control. The range of automatically readable film speeds extends from ISO 25/15° to ISO 5000/38°. The Dynax 8000i can also read the length of the film from the coding.

However, this is not all; the Dynax 8000i is the only camera that has an ISO value memory. This facility is particularly useful for photographers who like to use their personal film speed settings for certain films, as it is quite usual for some photographers to under- or overexpose a film with a certain rating by a certain amount. If this change of film speed is not done by +/- correction but by the more convenient override of the ISO speed then this value remains in memory. If the next film that is loaded has the same film speed rating as the previous one that was corrected by the photographer, then the camera remembers the corrected value and applies it again for the next film. If a film with a different film speed is loaded then the corrected film speed setting is cancelled.

Manual Film Speed Setting

Films can be bought that have variable speed. Then there are photographers who load film from bulk supplies into their own, uncoded cassettes. Some photographers use a film under certain circumstances as if it had a different speed rating from the one that has been

For manual setting of film speed, press the film-speed button, marked **ISO** in the card door and select the desired speed by using the setting control. The selected speed is always displayed in the data panel. This facility is used either to program the speed for an uncoded film cassette or to override the automatically read-in speed of a DX-coded film.

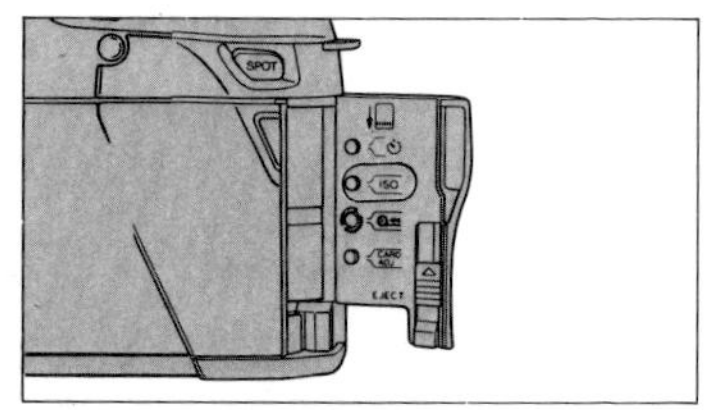

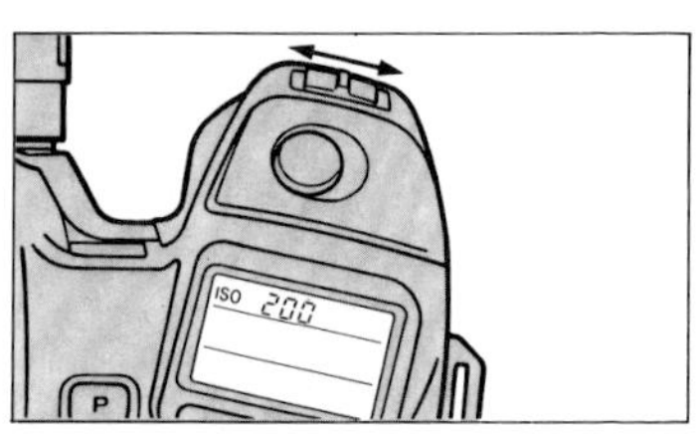

defined by the manufacturer, i.e. they "push" the film by forced development. The automatic reading-in of the film speed is a very convenient facility, but in the above situation it is anything but useful. However, the Dynax 8000i has the facility for manual setting, and override, of film speed.

To set the film speed manually, open the card door in the hand grip. Press the film-speed button **ISO** on the inside of the door and the speed of the film in use will be displayed in the LCD panel next to the ISO symbol. If you now push the setting control to the left, the speed will be reduced, pushing it to the right increases the speed. Each single activation of the setting control increases or decreases the film speed by a third of a stop. As soon as the required ISO value is reached, lightly press the release button to return to normal shooting mode. The selected, or automatically read-in, ISO value can always be read off by pressing the **ISO** button, alternatively you could just check through the film window where you can read off the speed of the loaded film, providing the setting has not been manually changed.

Intelligent Flash System

The Dynax 8000i intelligent flash system makes flash photography a pleasure. By coupling the flash system to the normal exposure metering system the camera is capable of automatically triggering a dedicated flashgun, such as the Minolta program flash 3200i, 2000i and 5200i, whenever poor lighting or backlit situations demand. When shooting in program mode the Dynax 8000i will automatically activate the flash whenever the lighting conditions necessitate it (as fill-in flash as well as for backlit subjects). The exposure metering analyses the situation and ensures that the backlit character of the picture is retained by metering the amount of flash accordingly. The Dynax 8000i is thus capable of automatically adjusting the balance

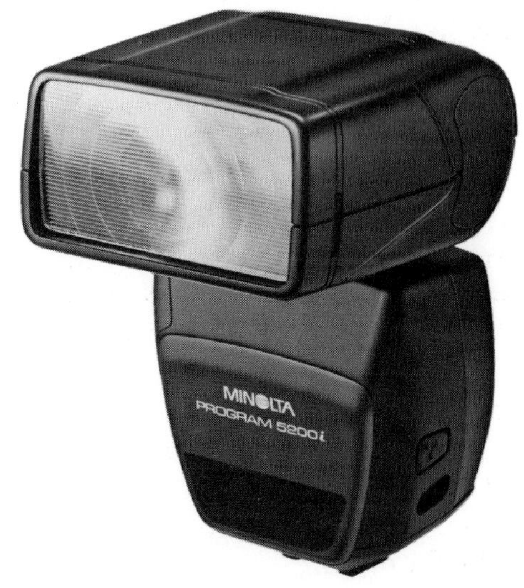

Minolta Program Flash 5200i:
A very powerful and particularly versatile unit for the Minolta Dynax 8000i.

between background and foreground to achieve a natural effect.

The automatic triggering of the flash can be suppressed by switching the flash off. This is done by pressing the on/off button at the back of the flashgun. The flashgun can be switched on again either by pressing the program reset button **P**, on the camera, or again pressing the on/off button on the flashgun.

The TTL direct metering system of the Dynax 8000i controls the flash duration automatically in all these functions. A silicon photo diode in the camera's pentaprism registers the strength of the flash illumination directly from the light reflected off the surface of the film. The fast flash synchronization speed of 1/200 sec is automatically set in **A** and **M** shooting modes, and in the **P** mode when the program decides whether flash should be used. In fact the speed will be set to 1/200 sec in **M** only if previously set to a higher speed. If lower, it will stay at that speed.

An ideal travelling companion: the Minolta AF 70-210mm, f/3.5-4.5 zoom – a very compact lens opening up different perspectives with easy framing. ⇨

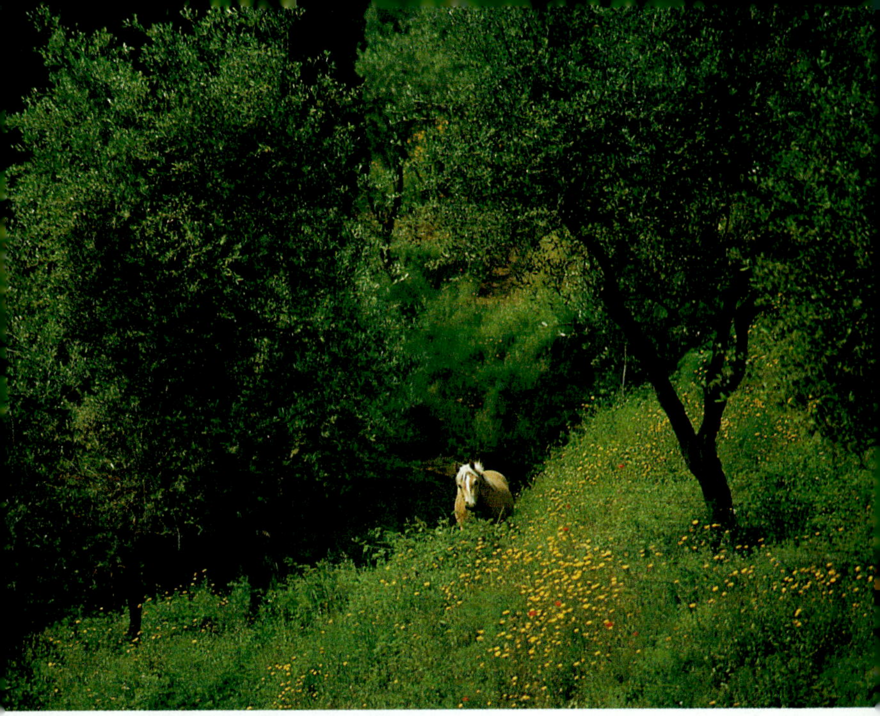

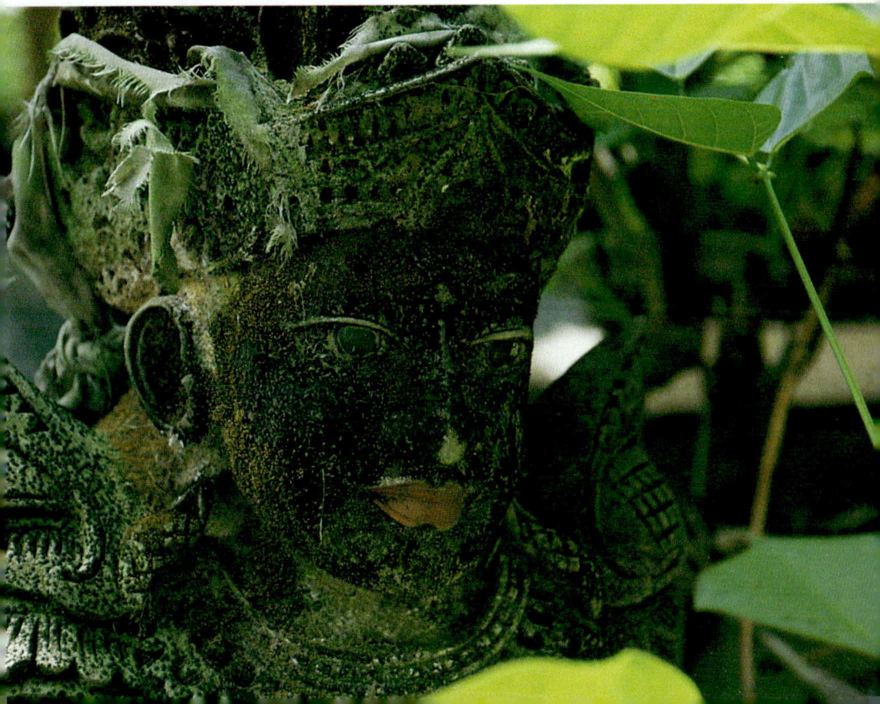

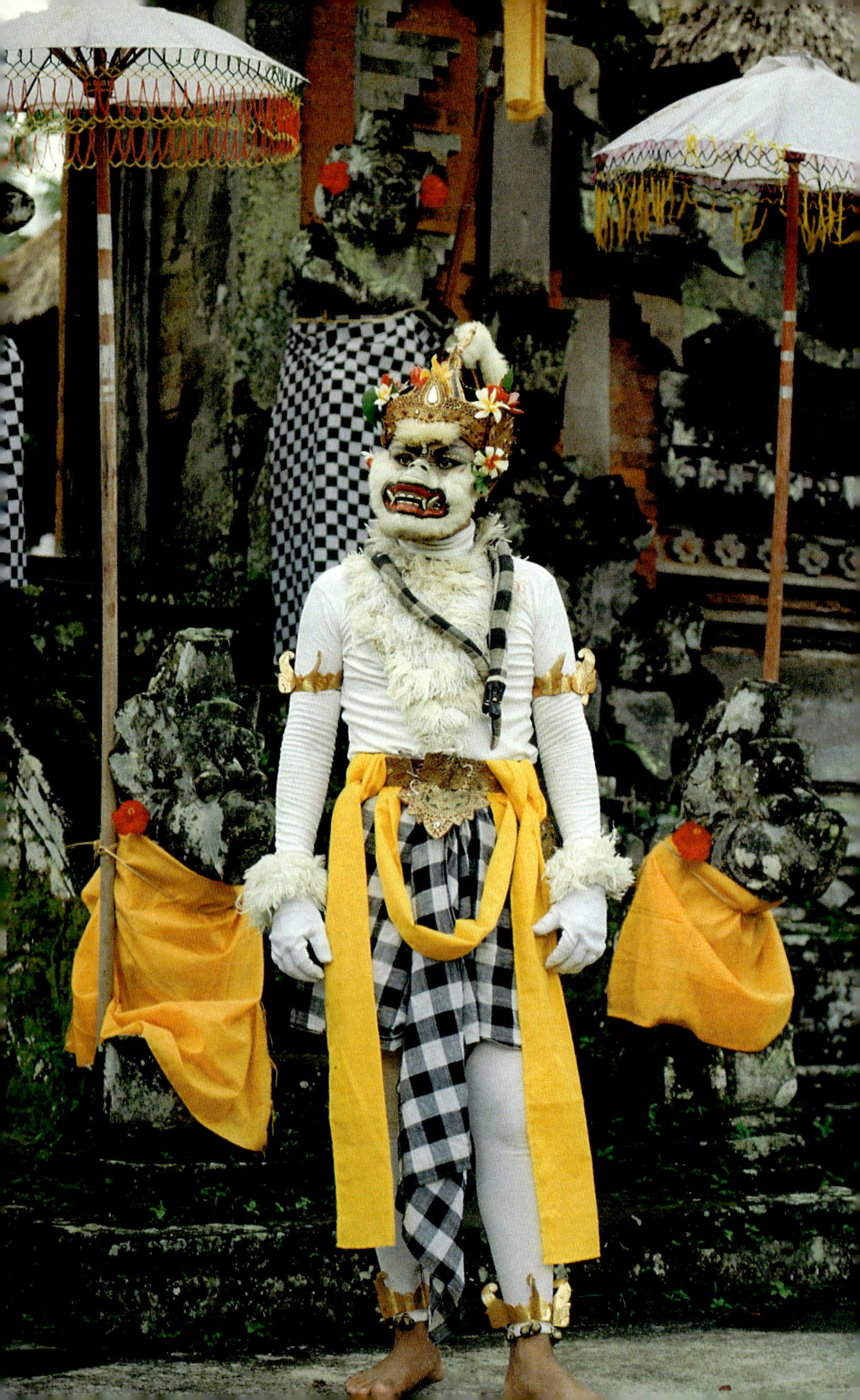

New Accessory Shoe

Accessory shoes used to be fitted with one centre contact to connect the flashgun. Modern cameras have additional contacts to allow automatic setting of flash synchronization speed and TTL flash metering. Since the introduction of the Minolta 7000, accessory shoes have been equipped with contacts to activate the AF Illuminator and the automatic adjustment of the zoom reflector setting and focal length of the lens.

It is possible to use previous Minolta program flashguns, such as, for example, the 1800 AF, the 2800 AF and the 4000 AF, and also the Macro Flash 1200 AF but you will need flash adaptor FS 1100. With this the TTL direct flash metering on the film surface and the flash function displays in the viewfinder will work perfectly. A function that does not work is the AF Illuminator. Instead, the Dynax 8000i will emit a metering light from its integrated AF Illuminator. This allows automatic focusing in complete darkness up to a distance of nine metres. However, this distance is approximate as it depends on the reflectivity of the subject and the prevailing lighting conditions.

⇦ *This is an ideal subject for Highlight / Shadow Control Card. In this case the light area, the light-coloured part of the costume, was measured.*

Another important flash function, the automatically-controlled fill-in flash in program mode, is not possible with these older flashguns. This function is only offered with the specially developed dedicated program flashguns 2000i, 3200i and the very powerful 5200i.

In addition the Minolta Dynax 8000i has a P.C. synchronizing socket. This allows connection of powerful non-program "Hammerhead" flash as well as studio flash units.

Photography with Dedicated Program Flashguns

As mentioned above, earlier flashguns for the Minolta autofocus 1000 series SLR cameras are suitable for use with the Dynax 8000i with some restrictions. The Minolta program flashguns 2000i, 3200i and 5200i, however, can only be used with cameras of the Dynax generation. Through the perfect co-operation between camera and flashgun it is possible to perform the most intricate flash photography of a professional standard. The intelligent flash control within the Dynax 8000i is capable of making the decision as to whether flash illumination is necessary or desirable and controls the correct amount of flash illumination, based on the flash illumination measured through the lens. Then there is the fill-in flash program that will ensure that excessively dark subject areas are illuminated, while the background retains its natural appearance.

To set the camera to program flash mode is easy; simply attach the flashgun to the accessory shoe and press the program reset button **P**. There are hardly

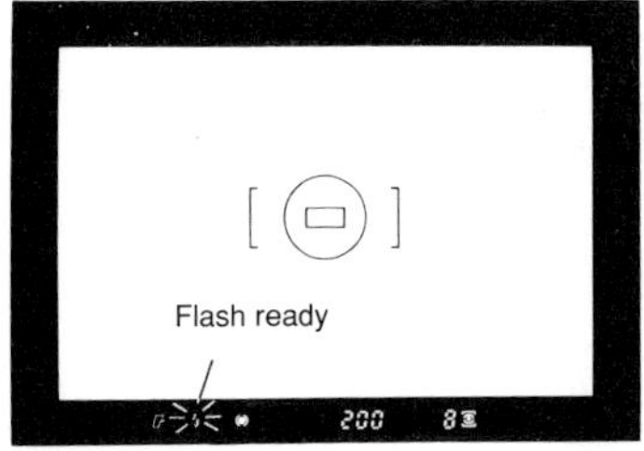

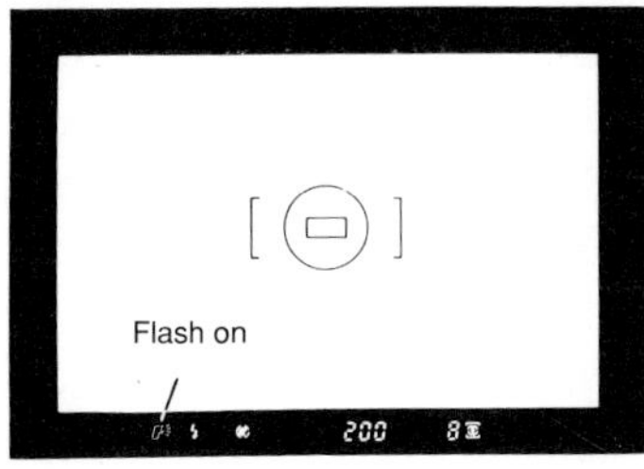

If a flash is attached, both flash-on and flash-ready symbols are displayed in the viewfinder.

any settings that need to be made on the flashgun itself, apart from the **ON/OFF** button, which is set of **OFF** to override the automatic function of the flashgun, and in the case of the 3200i the button for reduced output. However, the more powerful Minolta program flash 5200i has several operating elements to control its wealth of functions. In the bottom row between the **ON/OFF** and **TEST** buttons there is a another button, marked **MENU,** which is used to alternate between two function levels. The grey rubberised buttons in the top row control and correct a variety of functions. The button on the far left, **LIGHT/MULTI,** is used to switch on the illumination of the LCD panel and the stroboscope function, which is a series of flashes during a long exposure. The button next to it, **TTL-M/FREQ,** selects either automatic or manual operation. The same button can also be used to select the flash frequency of 50, 30, 10, 5, 3, 2 or 1 Hz. The third button, **ZOOM/REPS,** is used for motorized zoom adjustment and the number of stroboscopic flashes. It is possible to select frame frequencies of 10, 7, 5, 4, 3, 2 or unlimited flashes per frame. The button on the far right, **LEVEL/RATIO,** is used to select the output of the flash (1/1, 1/2, 1/4, 1/8, 1/16, 1/32) or for selecting the relative output if more than one flash is connected.

All the data and functions that are programmed by these buttons appear in the LCD panel. In the top row **OFF, ON, AUTO ON** and **OK** appear for sufficient flash output. In normal operation it will show the focal length setting for the zoom reflector, the flash range, the output and the automatic or manual setting of the zoom reflector. The flash range can be displayed either in imperial or metric units - selected via a switch in the battery compartment.

The Minolta program flash 5200i has a maximum guide number of 52 at ISO 100/21° at the 85mm zoom setting, and 42 at the 50mm setting. The flash range is 30 metres with an 50mm,f/1.4 lens. It is powered by four AA-size batteries or equal size rechargeable batteries. A fresh set of batteries should be sufficient for between 100 and 3,500 flashes with flashing rates from 0.2 to 11 seconds, the actual number being dependent on the shooting distance. It is also possible to connect this flash unit to an external power source which is available as an accessory.

The integrated AF Illuminator is perfectly adjusted for use with the multi-sensor AF system of the Dynax 8000i. Presented with a dark subject, or subject without strong contrasts, it will automatically emit three flashes to provide patterns for the camera to focus on. One flash projects a vertical pattern, to be read by the central AF sensor. The other two flashes project horizontal patterns that assist the two lateral AF sensors in their task. The AF Illuminator emits a tight beam of

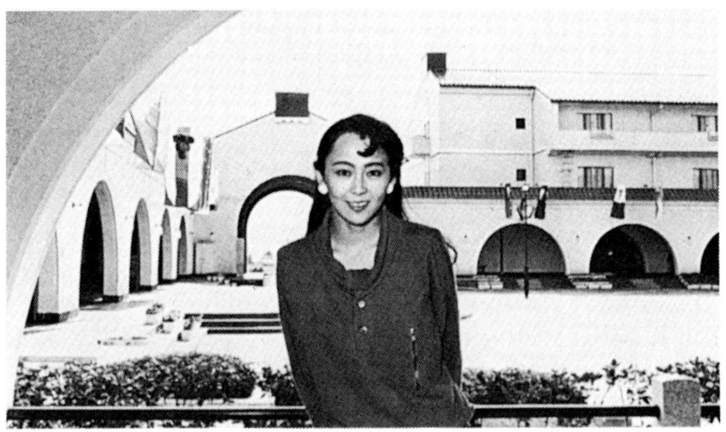

With fill-in flash.

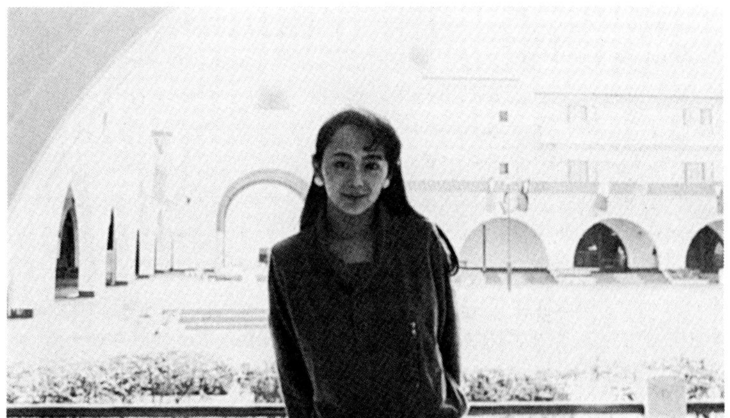

Without fill-in flash.

very bright light with a range of about 9 metres in complete darkness. This corresponds to the range of the integrated AF Illuminator of the Minolta Dynax 8000i.

The reflector of the Program Flash 5200i has an internal zoom-control motor, which adjusts the illumination angle automatically for the focal length of the attached lens. The necessary data for the focal length of the lens are transferred by the ROM chips which are integrated in every Minolta AF lens. The flash reflector automatically follows the focal length setting of an attached zoom lens within the limits of 24 to 85mm. It is possible to use the flash also with longer focal length lenses but then the light beam emitted by the flash will cover a wider angle of view than that of the lens. The Minolta Program Flash 5200i is capable of illuminating a much wider angle of view than the 3200i, which only covers an angle of view of 28 to 85mm. The guide number of the flashgun varies with the illumination angle - for a 24mm lens it is 28, for a 28mm lens it is 32, for a 35mm 36, for the 50mm 42 and for an 85mm lens it is 52. The guide numbers stated here refer to a film speed of ISO 100/21° and are stated in metres.

What is even more important than the guide number of the flashgun is the facility to manually adjust the zoom reflector (24mm, 28mm, 35mm, 50mm, 70mm and 85mm). This is useful when you are using indirect flash, for example when the flash reflector is pointed against the ceiling to soften the flash and avoid shadows. To ensure that the subject is completely illuminated and the light is as soft as possible the reflector should be set for a much shorter focal length than is actually attached to the camera. It is generally thought advantageous to set the zoom reflector wider by about two focal length settings. The high guide number of the 5200i comes in very useful for this. The reflector itself can be pointed upwards or to the right through 90° and through 180° to the left. When bouncing the light from a surface ensure that it is not highly coloured otherwise the light bounced back will lend the subject an unnatural colouring, but with the accessory Bounce Reflector III Set you can avoid this problem.

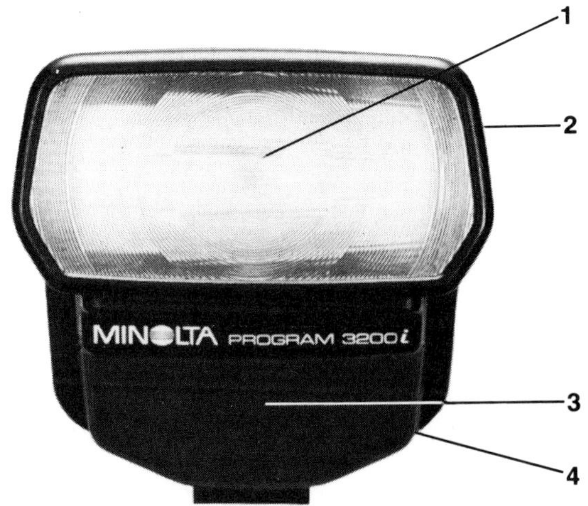

Minolta program flash 3200i: 1. flash reflector 2. internal motorized zoom reflector 3. AF illuminator 4. accessory shoe release 5. battery cover 6. program mode flash signal 7. on/off button 8. flash-ready symbol 9. output level selector 10. mounting foot

The Minolta Program Flash 3200i has been specially designed for the Dynax generation of cameras. All important functions are automatically controlled by the camera. The internal motorized zoom reflector adjusts the illumination angle to suit lenses from 28mm to 85mm focal length.

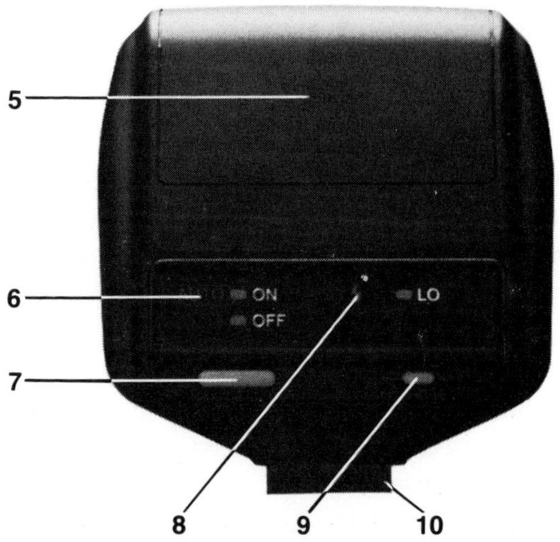

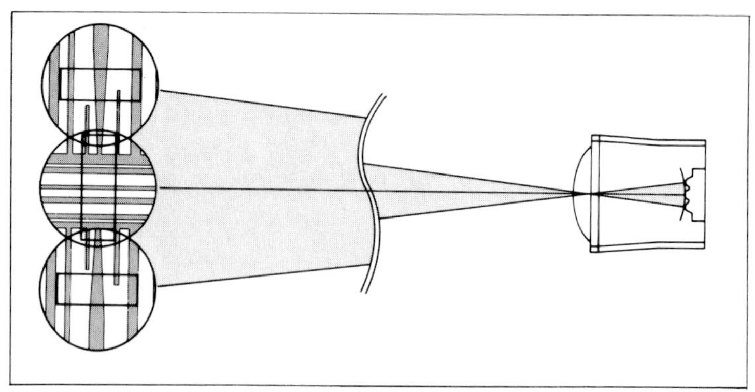

The AF illuminator of the program flash 3200i projects two vertical pattern and one horizontal pattern onto the subject to assist the autofocus system in dim lighting.

The Program Flash 5200i has an accessory socket for attaching a second flashgun of the "i" series. The flash output of the two units can be automatically controlled in a ratio of 1:2 or 2:1 by the **LEVEL/RATIO** button. It is possible to attach up to three flashguns of the "i" series by triple connector TC1000.

Program Flash 2000i, 3200i and 5200i all use an advanced electronic system for precise control of flash duration. These are the very first flashguns with an IGBT (Insulated Gate Bipolar Transistor) system. Compared with conventional thyristor control, this newly-developed system is capable of instantly switching the flash on and off. This is a considerable step forward in precise flash control. An additional advantage is that the flash construction requires 30% fewer parts. Consequently it is not only more reliable and precise, its construction is lighter and more compact. The flash charge is stored in two capacitors. The required flash output for correct exposure is calculated by the camera computer after the focus has been set. They take account of the subject distance, film speed

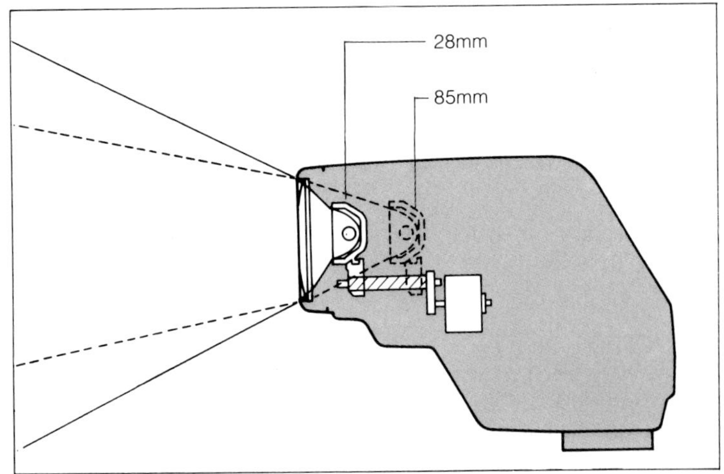

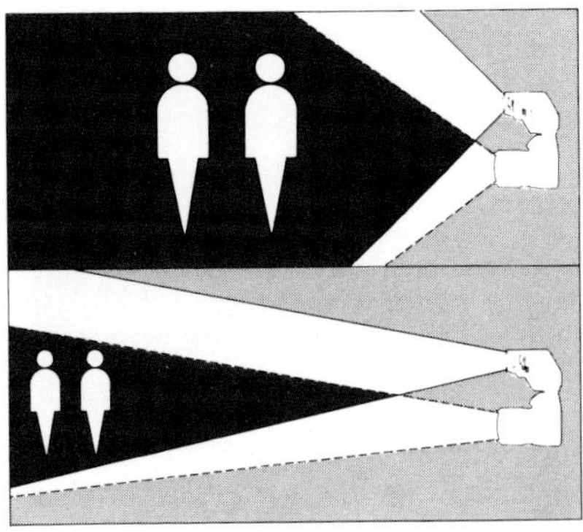

The internal zoom reflector of the Program Flash 3200i automatically adjusts its angle of view to the focal length of the lens used. Focal length range is between 28mm and 85mm.

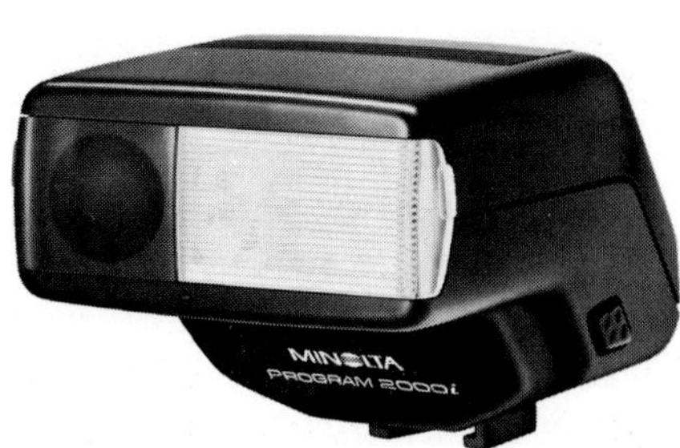

Minolta Program Flash 2000i.

and selected focal length. The two capacitors are charged, one after the other. As soon as they are sufficiently charged for the exposure requirements, the charging process is automatically terminated and the flash-ready symbol in the viewfinder starts to flash. For many shooting situations the charge of just one capacitor is quite sufficient and by this arrangement the flash recycling time of the Program Flash 5200i, and also the 3200i, is half that of conventional flashguns.

As well as displaying the flash-ready symbol, the viewfinder of the Dynax 8000i also confirms the correct amount of flash and whether the flashgun has been automatically activated by the camera.

Rapid Flash Sequences

Setting the Dynax 8000i to aperture priority or manual mode, reduced power from 1/1, 1/2, 1/4, 1/8, 1/16 to 1/32 can be set on the Program Flash 5200i by pressing the **LEVEL/RATIO** button. In this mode you can shoot flash sequences of up to three frames per second with reduced flash output. This corresponds approximately to the shooting rate of the Dynax 8000i in continuous mode.

Flash In Program Mode

As mentioned previously, the flash program mode is activated by attaching the Program Flash 5200i and pressing the program reset button **P.** In this mode the Dynax 8000i will automatically activate the flashgun and select the flash sync speed and aperture.

The camera also decides whether strong subject contrasts, for example in the case of backlit subjects, should be filled in, or if the lighting conditions demand the use of the flash. Depending on the focal length of the attached lens or the zoom setting, the automatic flash control adjusts the flash synchronization speed, which ranges from 1/20 to 1/200 sec for the Dynax 8000i.

The synchronization speed available on the Dynax 8000i is still not fast enough to take flash photographs in daylight of fast action scenes without speed-blur, but normal movements can be accommodated without any problem.

The camera can recognize whether the subject is uniformly lit or is positioned against a strong light source. When the flash is used to lighten backlit subjects, the camera will measure the background lighting and allow just enough flash output to fill-in the main subject in the foreground, reducing the contrast without destroying the backlit character of the picture.

It is not possible to reduce the flash output for fast flashing rates in program mode. When shooting in shutter speed priority the camera functions as in program mode. The flash synchronization speed is automatically selected by the Dynax 8000i and cannot be manually selected.

Flash with Aperture Priority Mode

Flash can also be used in automatic mode with the camera in aperture priority mode. In this mode the photographer may preselect any suitable aperture value. This mode is particularly useful if the depth of field is an important consideration for the composition.

The aperture plays an important role, particularly when taking backlit pictures. Often it is desirable to show the background as a blurred and undefined backdrop, which requires a wide open aperture. Large apertures could also be necessary to maximise the range of the flash. In the close range, on the other hand, a small aperture may be necessary to increase the depth of field. In this mode the photographer can use the appropriate aperture to suit the requirements of the subject and the flash control will take care of the appropriate flash output. The flash synchronization speed, on the other hand, will always be set by the camera at 1/200 sec. Slower flash synchronization speeds may be obtained by metering the background. Press and hold the **SPOT** button, at the rear of the camera. This metered exposure time will be retained and used for the flash shot. Using this procedure prevents the background being lost in absolute blackness when shooting at night. You need not worry about camera shake in this instance, as the very short flash illumination time will freeze the subject on the film, although the background might suffer from camera shake if the camera is hand held.

Flash with Manual Exposure

The automatic flash control works also if the photographer preselects aperture and shutter speed manually. If a preselected shutter speed, faster than 1/200 sec, is chosen by mistake, then the Dynax 8000i will override this setting. Shutter speeds of up to 30 sec may be used and will be retained. Cameras with a focal plane shutter can only use a limited range of shutter speeds for correct flash illumination. Focal plane shutters, which are universally used in all modern SLR cameras, effect their exposure times by the movement of two blinds made up of a system of blades that expose the film. Shutter speeds of 1/200 sec and faster are formed by the movement across the film plane of a slit of varying widths outlined by the two shutter blinds, i.e. only part of the frame is exposed at any one time. This works as follows: The first shutter blind starts to move across the film plane, exposing part of the negative and the second blind follows before the first blind has reached the other side; therefore the whole area is never completely exposed at any one time. Because the slit takes longer to traverse the film plane than the duration of the flash, the latter will therefore only illuminate part of the frame, i.e. only for the instant the flash is triggered.

The situation is different for slower shutter speeds. In this case the first blind exposes the frame completely before the second starts to follow. Now the flash can be triggered any time, usually immediately after the first blind reaches the other side and the whole picture area will be illuminated.

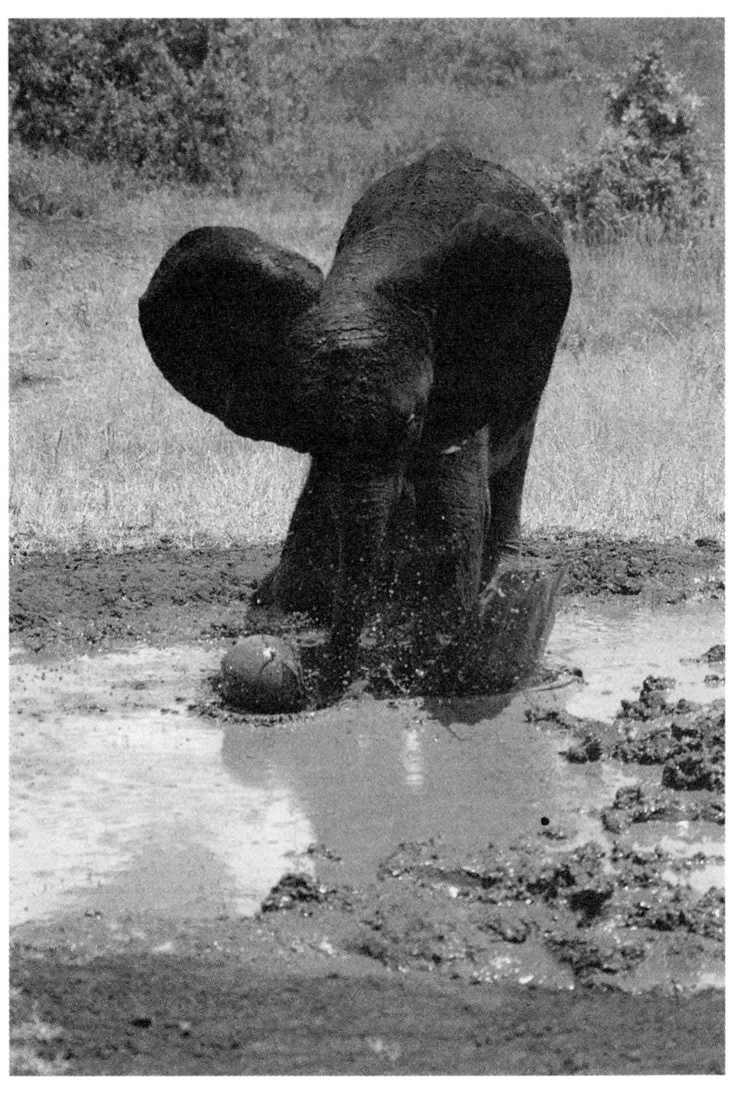

This baby elephant looks very charming and harmless. However, it is best to keep a respectful distance. The ideal equipment: Dynax 8000i with AF 100-300mm, f/4, 5-5.6 zoom.

The AF Lens Program

One of the most important advantages of SLR cameras is be able to use one camera body with a range of different lenses. The photographer can choose the most suitable focal length and other special characteristics for a given task. The Minolta AF system now offers over 30 lenses and converters, covering a wide range from the fisheye to the 600mm super telephoto. All these may be used with the Dynax 8000i, together with a wide range of independent makers' lenses for Minolta AF cameras and manufactured under licence from Minolta and using chips purchased from Minolta. Such lenses are fully compatible with the Dynax 8000i. However, some manufacturers produce lenses with a Minolta AF-type bayonet, but using chips of non-Minolta origin. These lenses may not be usable with

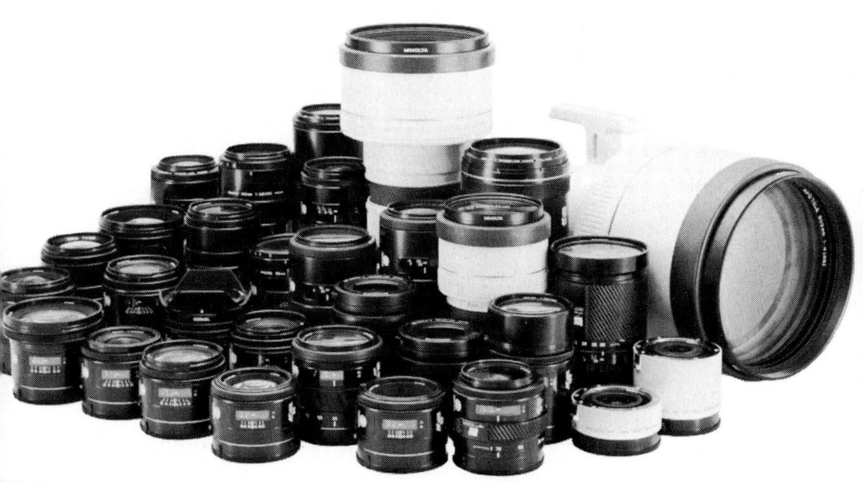

the Dynax without some kind of modification.

The ROM (read only memory) integrated circuits in the Minolta AF lenses ensure the perfect co-operation between camera and lens. Without these circuits the camera computer would not be able to control either the exposure or the autofocus. The information about focal length, speed, and aperture range, of the attached lens is stored in the ROM-integrated circuit. This is automatically read into the camera computer and forms the basis for the camera metering data and the resulting control impulses. This allows the camera computer to continuously adjust, say, the exposure, if the attached lens is a zoom and the focal length is changed, or the changed illumination angle of the integrated zoom reflector in the Program Flash 3200i or 5200i, in line with the changing focal lengths. This high level of automation would not be possible without the continuous exchange of data between camera and lens.

This also demonstrates the possible dangers of using an independent lens that has not been manufactured under Minolta licence. In an extreme case such an unsuitable lens could damage the camera's electronics. It is also likely that future changes to the central camera computer could upset the function of such lenses. An endeavour to save money by buying a cheaper lens could turn out quite an expensive business after all.

Why Interchangeable Lenses?

Changing lenses enhances the creative range of a SLR camera. By using different focal lengths it is possible to change the framing, or angle of view, without having to change the camera position.

We distinguish five different groups of lenses according to their focal lengths and special characteristics. These are the wide-angle, standard, telephoto, macro and zoom lenses.

Wide-angle lenses have a focal length of 35mm and shorter. Such lenses have a large angle of view and allow a wide view from a short shooting distance. The shorter the focal length, the wider the angle of view.

One special group within the wide-angle range is the fisheye lens with an angle of view of 180°. The special characteristic of these lenses is the strong barrel shaped distortion, i.e. any straight lines that do not run through the centre of the image are reproduced as curved, becoming more exaggerated the closer they are to the edge of the picture.

Standard lenses have a focal length of about 50mm. Their angle of view of 45° corresponds roughly to that of the human eye.

Telephoto lens have focal lengths from about 70-80mm upwards and they allow you to depict a subject which is at a certain distance filling the frame.

Macro lenses for the Dynax 8000i are available for 50mm and 100mm focal length; as well as the only AF Macro Zoom for reproduction ratios from 1:1 to 3:1. These are special lenses for subjects to be taken at close range. They are designed to show small subjects at a large scale of reproduction.

Zoom lenses provide continuous change of focal length within certain limits. This allows the framing and the reproduction ratio of a given subject to be varied without having to change the shooting position or lens. Great technical advances have been made in recent years in the field of zoom lens design. Not only have they become smaller and lighter, but their optical qualities are now comparable to lenses of fixed focal length. Zoom lenses therefore are very popular and the Minolta AF system includes 11 zooms with different focal length ranges. Five of these were specially developed for the Dynax generation of cameras.

Reproduction Scale and Perspective

Shooting distance and focal length determine how large a subject is represented on film. The relationship between subject size and reproduction size is called reproduction ratio. It is of no consequence to the reproduction ratio whether a subject at long distance is taken with a long focal length or from a short distance with a short focal length. The photographer can take one particular subject at the same reproduction ratio with different focal length lenses by varying his position. However, the actual pictures taken in this way will be considerably different from each other.

By changing the shooting position the perspective in the picture changes. By perspective we mean the relative sizes of objects at different distances from the camera position, and how a three-dimensional subject is represented on a two-dimensional surface. If the distance between camera and subject is changed then the relative sizes of the subject with different distances to the camera position will also change. The perspective is therefore not dependant on the focal length of the lens, only on the lens to subject distance. If we could enlarge photographs to any size, then we would not need to take telephoto pictures with long focal lengths, we could simply enlarge a section of the wide-angle view to obtain the required section in the necessary size. It would have the same perspective as the tel-

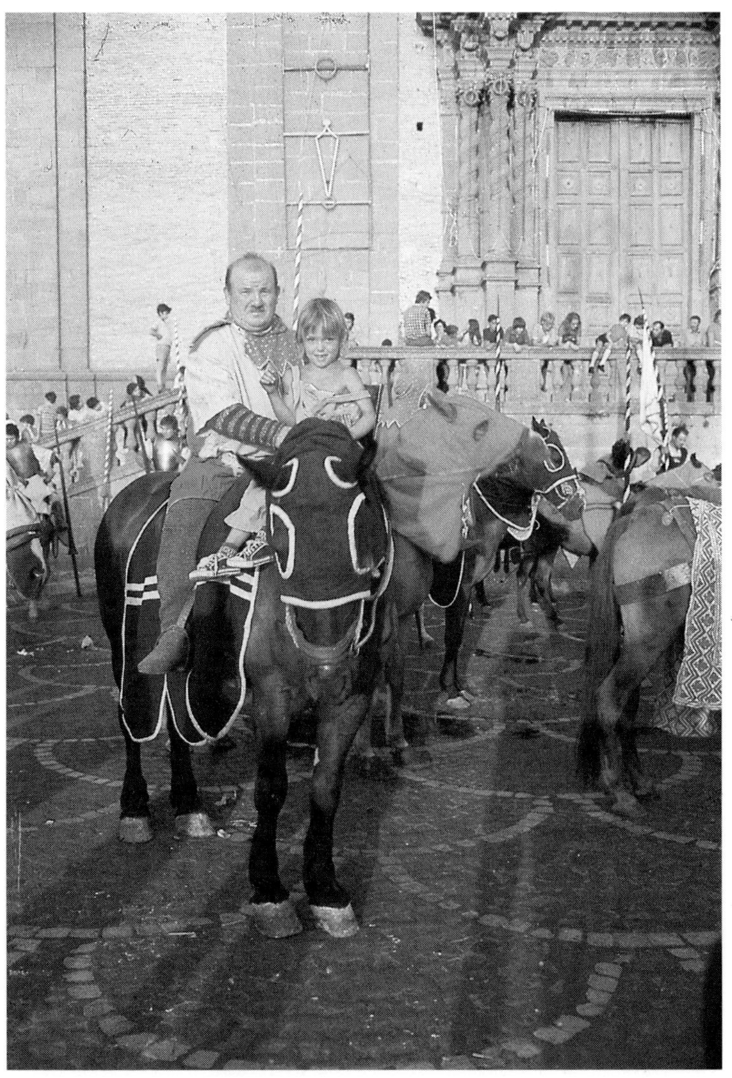

The Minolta AF 24-50mm, f/4 zoom is the ideal lens at close quarters to capture the activities of people at festivals and similar events.

ephoto view from the same shooting position. The shorter the shooting distance, the change in relative sizes becomes more noticeable.

AF Zoom Lenses

The new design of these lenses is characterised by extremely short focusing movements which increase their focusing speed dramatically compared with the older design.

The focusing speed has also been considerably improved. Because of the new software of the AF computer and the more powerful AF motor, the Dynax 8000i is capable of focusing much faster, even with the older style lenses, than the Minolta cameras of the previous generation. On the other hand the new zoom lenses can be used without restriction on the older Minolta AF cameras.

Through the use of the most modern methods of construction and new special materials, the new Minolta zoom lenses are extremely compact. In their class they are the smallest and lightest now available.

The centre-weighted average metering method was the correct choice for this scene. ⇨

The flower "portraits" on the following pages were taken with the Minolta AF 50mm, f/2.8 Macro. ⇨

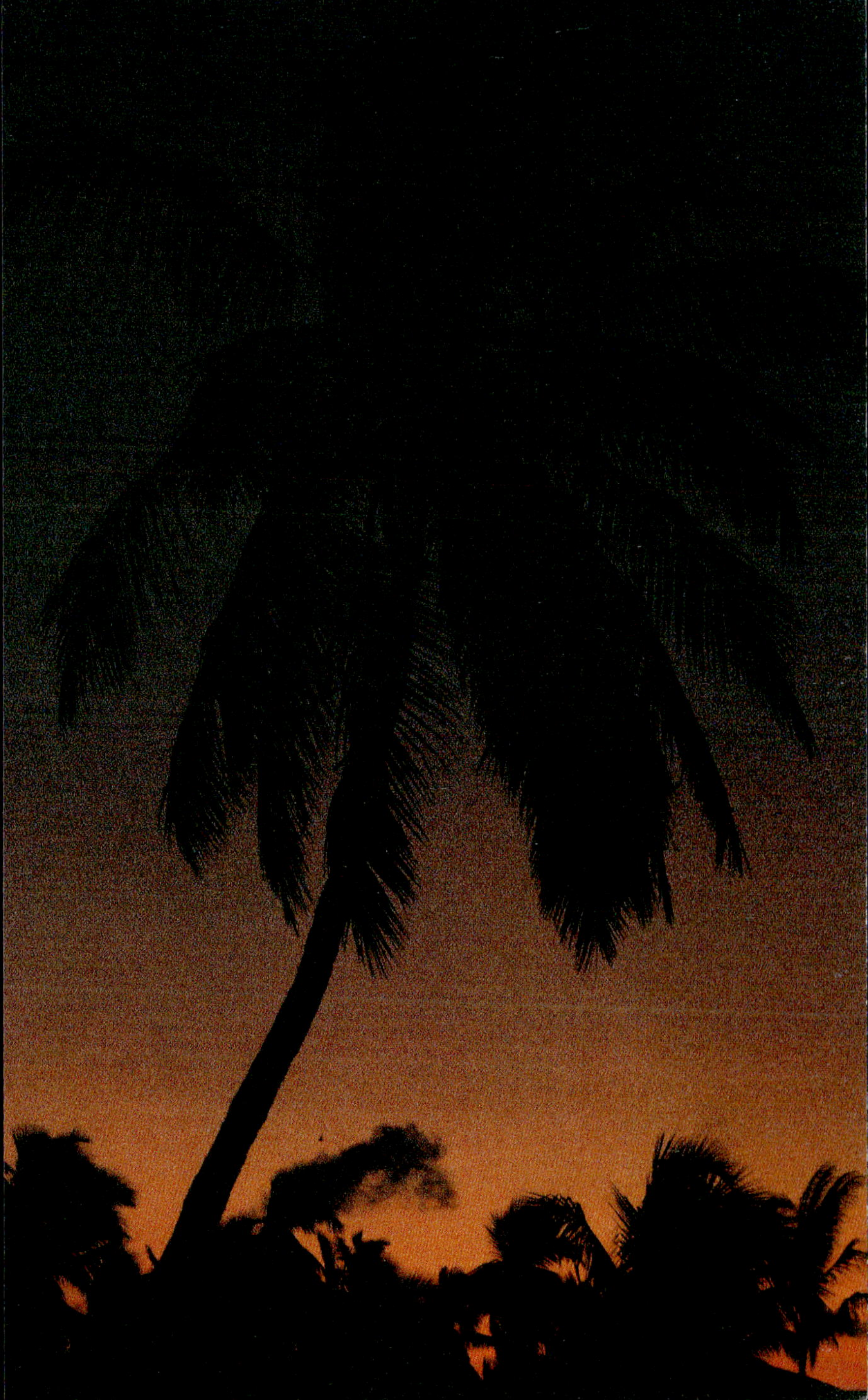

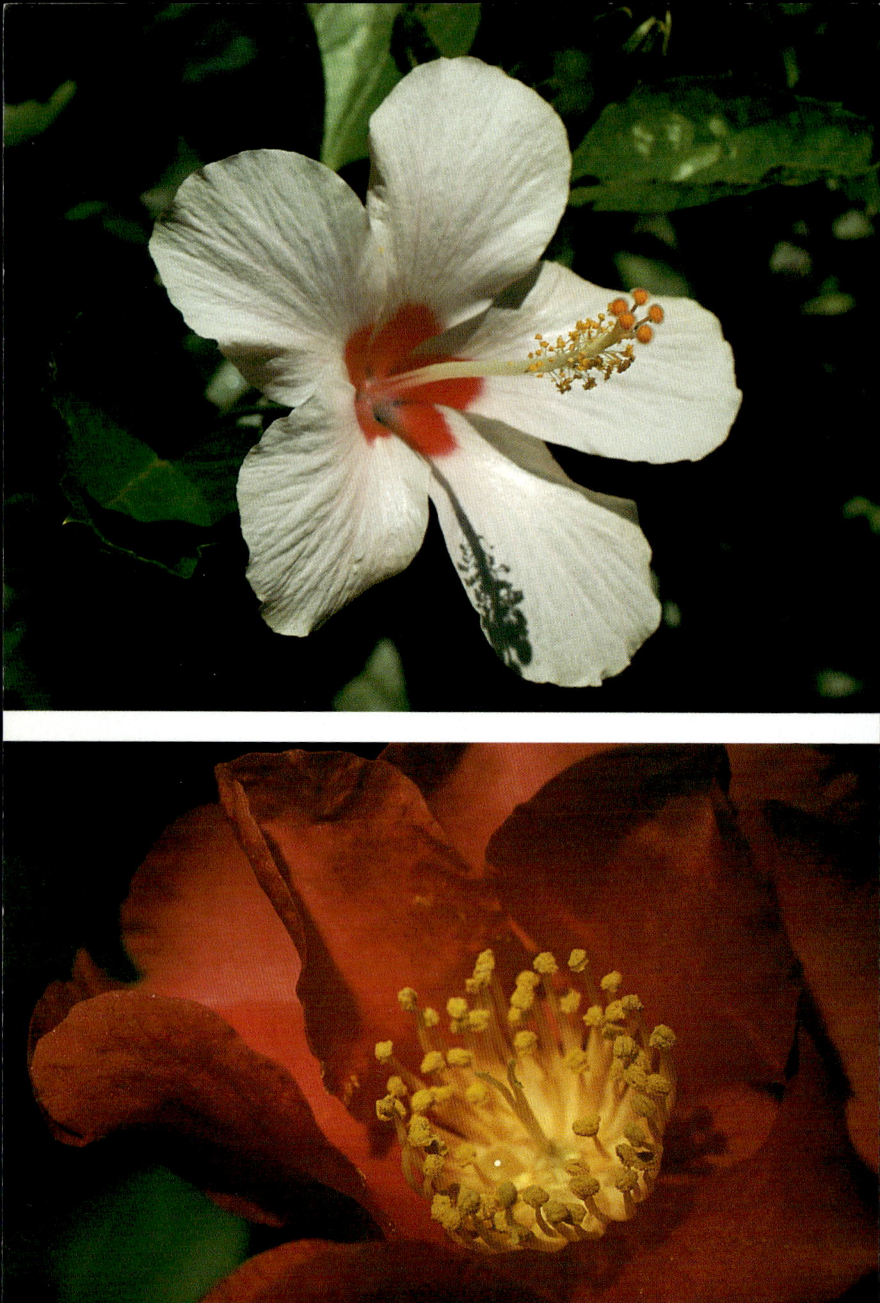

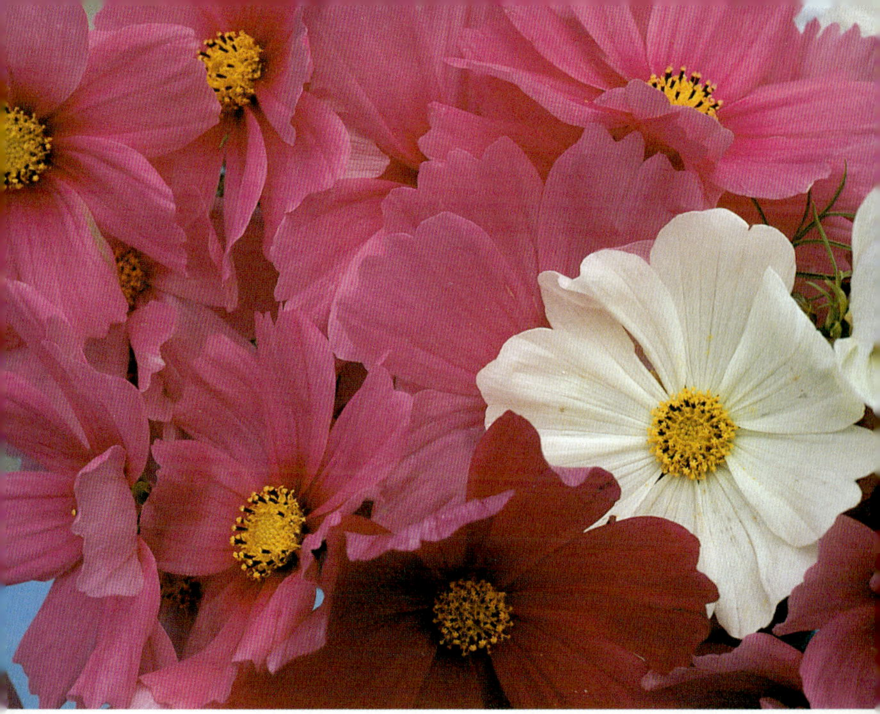

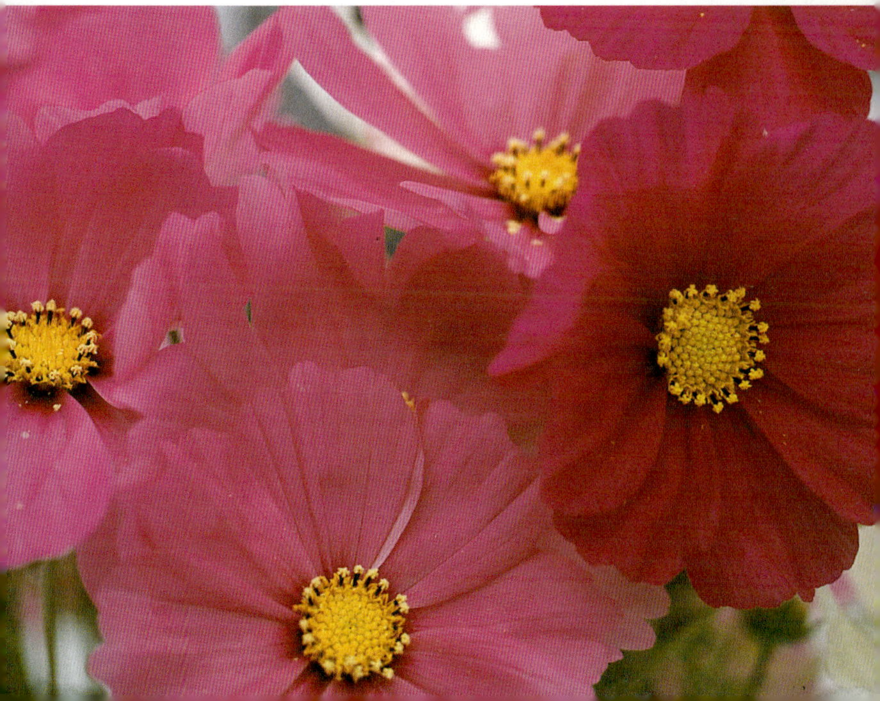

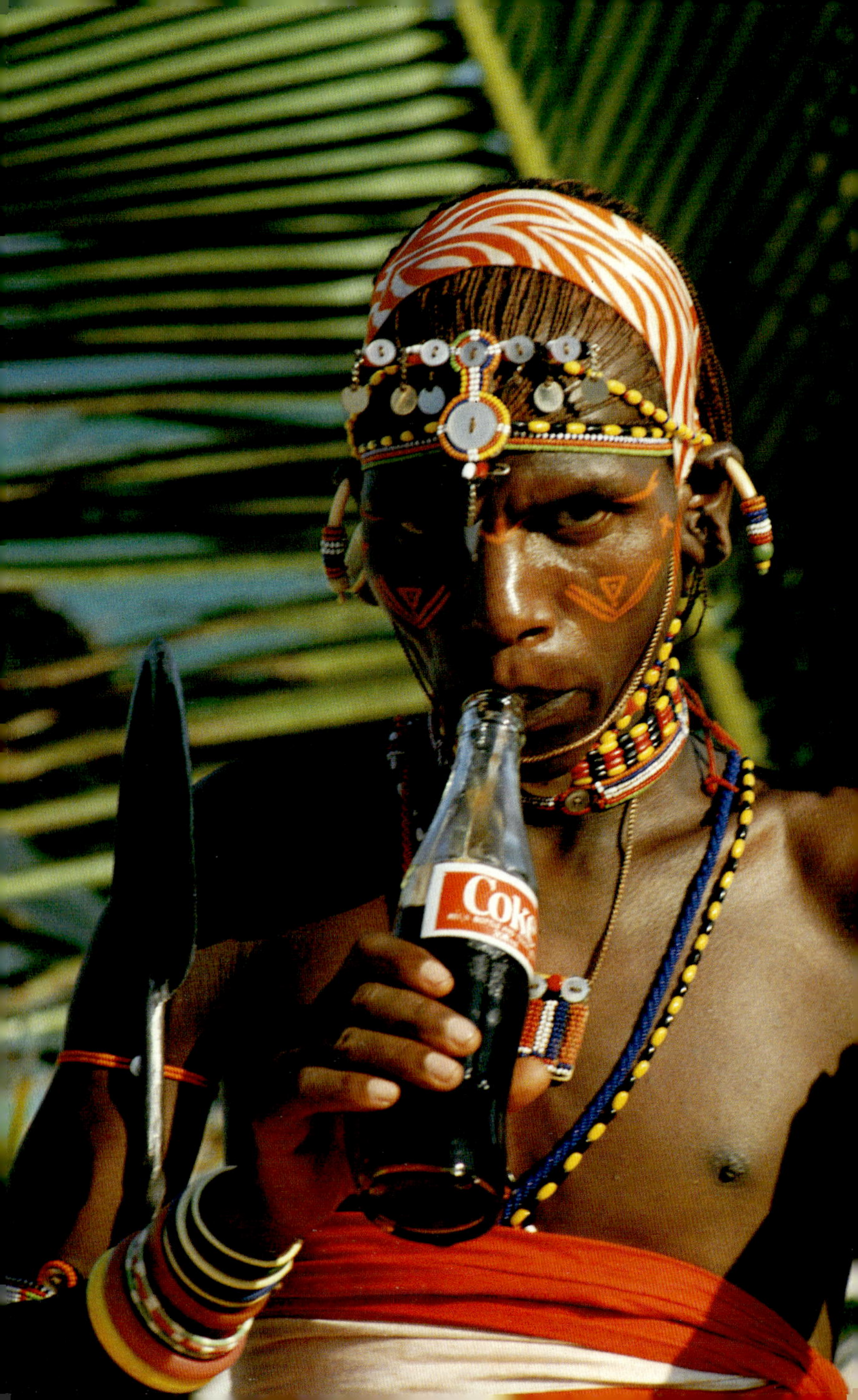
Coke

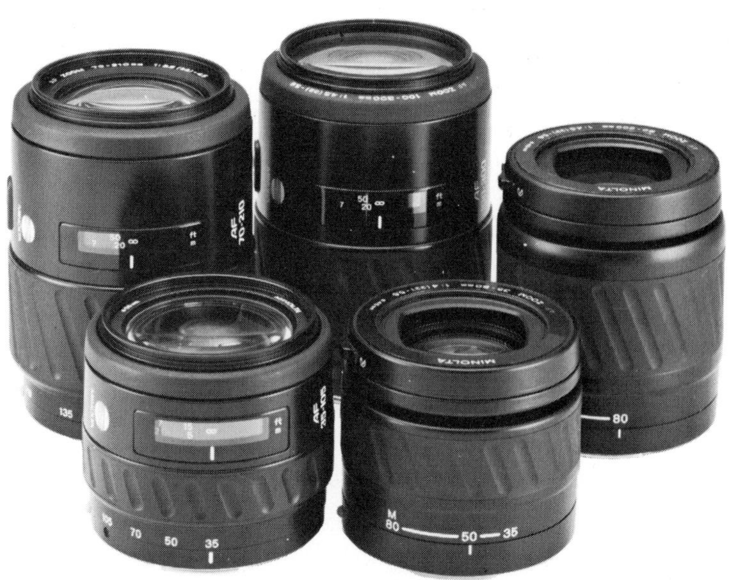

The five new Minolta AF zoom lenses are the most compact and lightest in their class. All five lenses have been developed to increase the automatic focusing speed with the new Dynax generation of cameras (8000i, 7000i, 5000i and 3000i), as well as the previous one.

⇦ *The Minolta AF 35-80mm zoom is very compact and handy with a wide range of applications from photo reportage to portraiture.*

The very short overall length is achieved thanks to the use of special aspherical elements which possess several curvatures. This does away with the necessity of having to use special elements to compensate for the lens error known as spherical aberration - a problem which used to be solved by combining mutually compensating diverging and converging elements. Aspherical lenses do not suffer from spherical aberrations because of the continuous change of the curvature of the lens surface, mainly towards the edge. The technical realization of this principle has been so difficult that most manufacturers have used these elements only in their most expensive lenses. The machine tools for producing aspherical elements have to work to much finer tolerances than those needed to produce conventional elements.

AF 35-80mm,f/4-5.6 zoom:
This is the smallest and lightest (200g) of the new AF zooms for the Dynax cameras and replaces the earlier 35-70mm,f/4. These focal lengths cover more than half of all photographic subjects that are generally photographed. From the group photograph to the portrait head, from the landscape to the snap of playing children taken from a discreet distance, all these are subjects that this lens will cover very conveniently. In the close range this lens can reach a reproduction ratio of 1:6.

The integrated lens cover protects the front element against dirt, dust and scratches. It is also very handy when changing lenses, preventing accidental touching of the front element, or loss of the lens cap. Opening and closing of the lens is simply and quickly done by pushing the little slider at the side of the lens which moves the laminal plates, more or less according to the principle of a cigar cutter, at the same time the housing

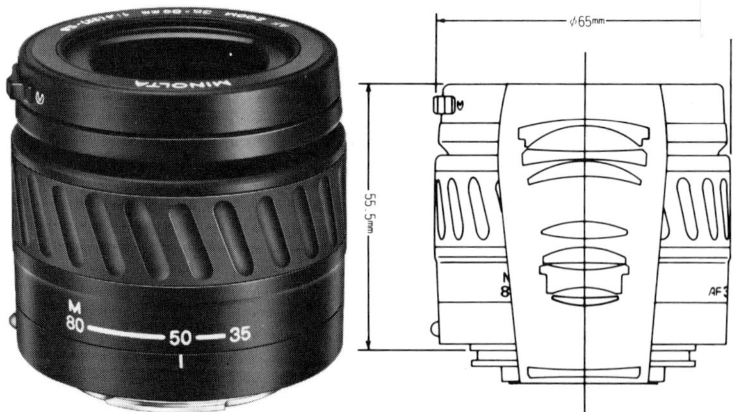

The Minolta AF 35-80mm f/4-5.6 zoom: this is the smallest lens of this specification on the market. The use of an aspherical element makes it particularly light whilst ensuring excellent reproduction quality. The front cover is integrated.

containing this mechanism acts as a lens hood.

The diameter of the filter thread is very small. It measures only 46mm and filters with this diameter are naturally cheaper than the larger ones.

For changing the focal length you now have a wide rubber cover ring, affording a good grip. There is a rather narrow focusing ring at the front of the lens for manual focusing. This has no special easy-grip surface but as you will use it only very rarely this should not be a problem. Because of its particular compact and light construction this lens is particularly useful as a universal one.

AF 35-105mm,f/3.5-4.5 zoom:
Despite the greater speed and large focal length range, this zoom is only 1.5mm longer than the 35-80mm zoom. It has an aspherical element which is the reason for its extremely compact construction. Compared with conventional designs it is about 40% lighter.

It covers a 3:1 range of focal lengths, is relatively fast and as such universally useful. If you also consider the macro setting, then you have a most useful and versatile lens that will be a most handy companion. The very short focusing movement ensures very exact focusing. The closest focusing distance is 85cm. At this distance it is possible to take close-ups with a reproduction scale of 1:6. It weighs 290g.

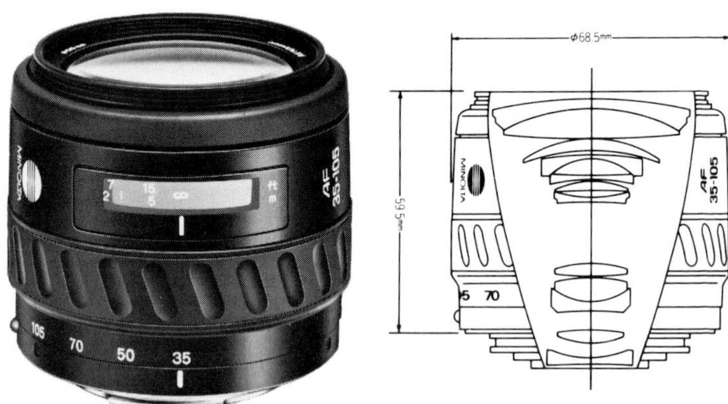

Minolta AF 35-105mm, f/3.5-5.6 zoom: the most compact lens of its class. Here too, an aspherical element ensures excellent quality at 40% of the weight of a conventionally designed comparable lens.

AF 80-200mm,f/4.5-5.6 zoom:

This zoom in the classical telephoto focal length range is the obvious companion to the 38-80mm zoom. Similar in its internal construction, it also possesses the integrated front element cover. It weighs only 390g and measures 78mm. These measurements make it one of the smallest and lightest in its class. It also has the extremely small filter diameter of only 46mm and employs the principle of double-tele zoom, which ensures particularly fast automatic focusing. Its lightweight and compact construction make it the ideal lens for travel photography. The shortest focusing distance is 1.5m, facilitating full format reproduction of even quite small objects. The largest reproduction scale with this lens is 1:6.

AF 70-210mm,f/3.5-4.5 zoom:
Despite covering a 3:1 range of focal lengths this telephoto zoom lens is relatively fast, allowing fast shutter speeds for rapid action photography without having to resort to very high-speed films even if the lighting conditions are not particularly good. This lens weighs 420g and measures 100mm.

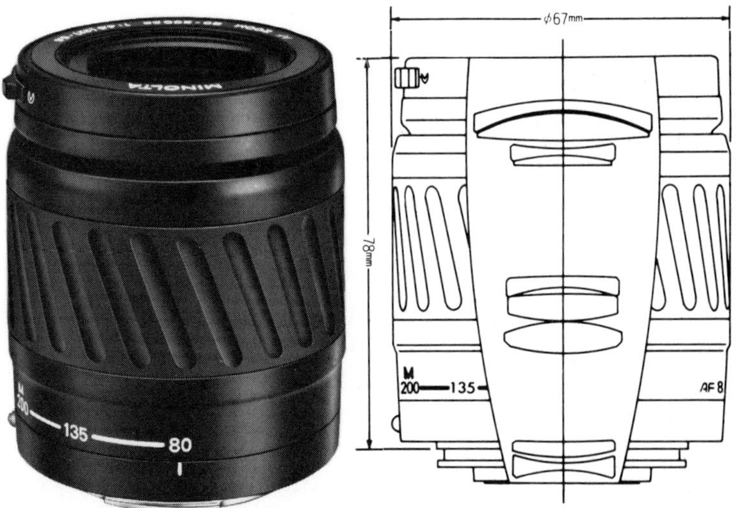

Minolta AF 80-200mm, f/4.5-5.6 zoom: this lens has been constructed according to the double tele zoom principle making is very compact. Integrated front cover.

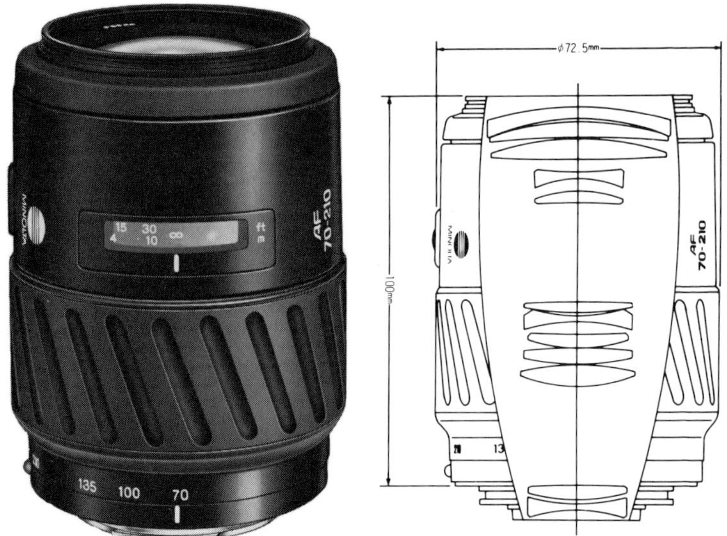

Minolta AF 70-210mm, f/3.4-4.5 zoom: the principle of a double tele zoom makes this an extremely compact and light lens. The integrated focus-stop button provides an additional facility.

One special characteristic of this lens is the focus-stop button. Pressing this button stops the focusing process and the release may be activated. This cancels the in-focus priority. Individual programming of the focus-stop facility, with the Customized Function Card and the Dynax 7000i, is not possible in combination with the Dynax 3000i or 5000i. With the 7000i the focus-stop button can be used to change over to continuous autofocus or to focusing by central AF target field. This is not possible with the Dynax 3000i or 5000i because they do not have a central AF target field.

The diameter of the filter thread of this lens is 55mm. The ring for focal length settings has an easy-grip rubber covering and the closest focusing distance is 1.1m.

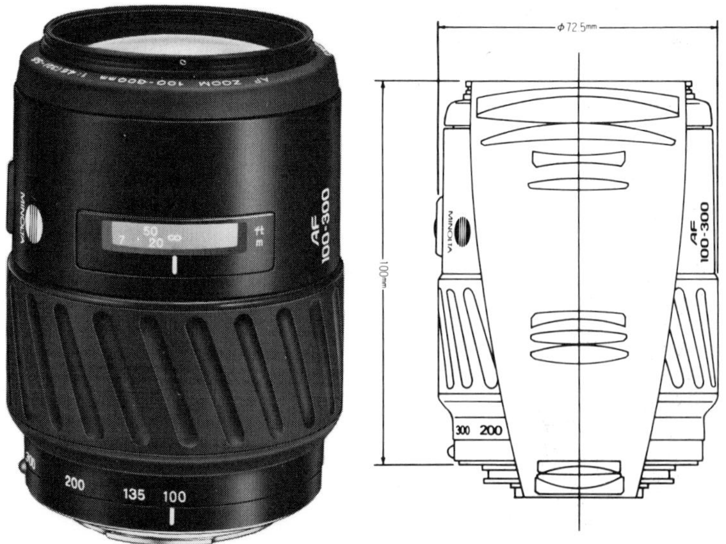

Minolta AF 100-300mm, f/4.5-5.6 zoom: a very compact tele zoom lens covering three focal lengths. Double tele zoom system with focus-stop button.

AF 100-300mm,f/4.5-5.6 zoom:

Sports, animal and landscape photography are the domain of this telephoto zoom lens with a 3:1 focal length range. Due to its ingenious construction it weights 10g less than the 70-210mm zoom but is the same length (78mm). It also employs the focus-stop button to override in-focus priority.

The filter diameter is 55mm, the shortest focusing distance is 1.5m and biggest reproduction ratio is 1:4. The extremely compact construction and light weight make it an ideal companion on any journey. With it and the 35-105mm zoom you can cover a very wide range of focal lengths. (100, 135, 180, 200 and 300mm).

Well-proven Minolta AF Zoom Lenses

Apart from the five lenses described above, which were specially developed for the introduction of the Dynax generation of cameras, and the AF Macro Zoom 3X, described in the chapter for Macro lenses, Minolta offers a further seven zoom lenses with different focal length ranges, all of which may be used without restriction with the Dynax 8000i. Considering this wide range of lenses no other camera manufacturer has a larger range of auto-focus lenses than Minolta.

AF 24-50mm,f/4 zoom:
This may be described as the real reportage lens. It is perfectly suited to catch the action at fun fairs, festivals, market places, or inside buildings. Then there are landscape and architectural photography, two applications that are perfectly served by this focal length range. The relatively fast speed of f/4 ensures a reasonable flash range in poor lighting conditions.

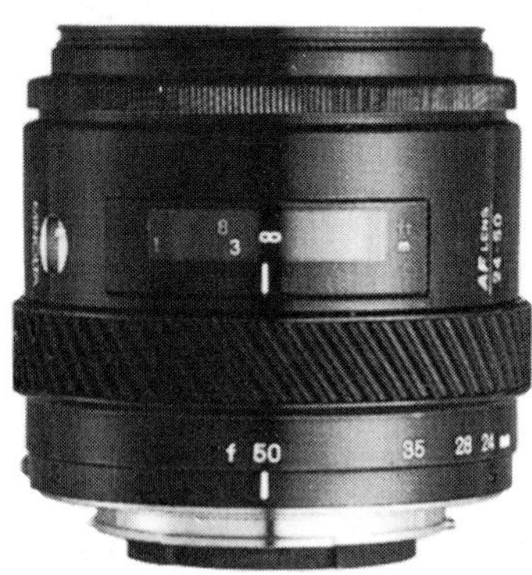

AF 25-50mm, f/4 zoom

This very handy zoom lens also contains one of the new aspherical elements, and thus possesses excellent optical qualities and very fast focusing characteristics. As it only weighs 285g and measures a mere 60mm it can accompany you anywhere without weighing you down. The filter size is 55mm.

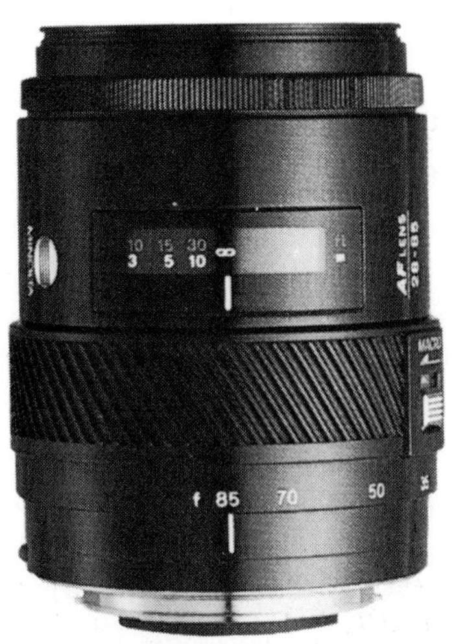

AF 28-85mm, f/3.5-4.5 zoom

AF 28-85mm,f/3.5-4.5 zoom:
Covering a 3:1 focal length range, from the wide-angle to the portrait telephoto, compared with the new construction zoom in this range, it has the advantage of extending the wide-angle range, making it much more versatile in restricted spaces. At festivals or in crowds, this is a very handy lens. It will serve you well for a

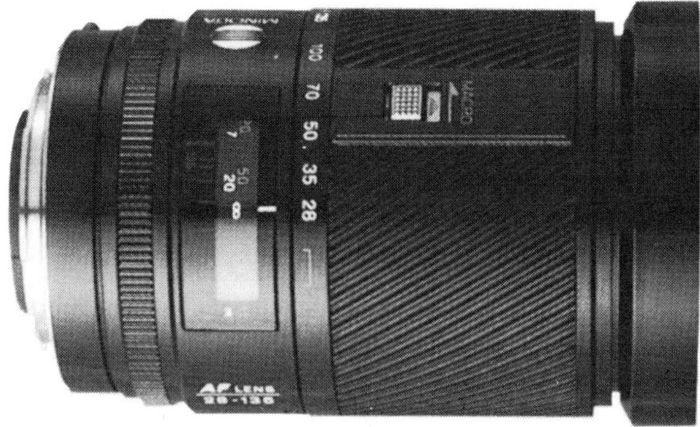

AF 28-135mm, f/4-4.5 zoom

variety of tasks from group photos to full format portraits. The relatively high speed makes it particularly suitable for fast snap shots and also for flash photography with medium to high speed films.

AF 28-135mm,f/4-4.5 zoom:
This lens covers an even wider section of the telephoto range. It weighs 750g and has also a bigger diameter than the 28-85mm. Whether you decide on the 28-85mm or the 28-135mm zoom lens, depends very much on which zoom lens you have chosen for the long range. If you cover the telephoto range with the 70-210mm zoom lens, then you would probably be best served by the 28-85mm for the standard zoom range. If your telephoto zoom is the 100-300mm, then I would recommend the 28-135mm.

AF 75-300mm,f/4.5-5.6 zoom:
This lens offers a bigger focal length range of 4:1 and another 25mm in the initial focal length than the new design 100-300mm, and is, as such, a very useful lens for animal and sports photography. But the very expensive construction utilises 13 elements in 11 groups, makes it twice as heavy and longer by 63.5mm than the

new 100-300mm zoom lens. One particular characteristic of this lens is the switch on the lens tube, which allows the distance range for focusing to be limited. There are two positions, one for the close range from 1.5m-3m, and a far distance from 4m-infinity. This provision decreases the focusing time as the lens does not need to travel the whole focusing distance.

AF 80-200mm,f/2.8 Apo zoom:
A heavy-weight amongst the AF zoom lenses, but a real optical marvel! It distinguishes itself by its extremely fast speed and high reproduction quality through the use of special AD glasses to correct for secondary spectrum. In its construction are a total of 16 elements arranged in 13 groups, which make themselves felt by

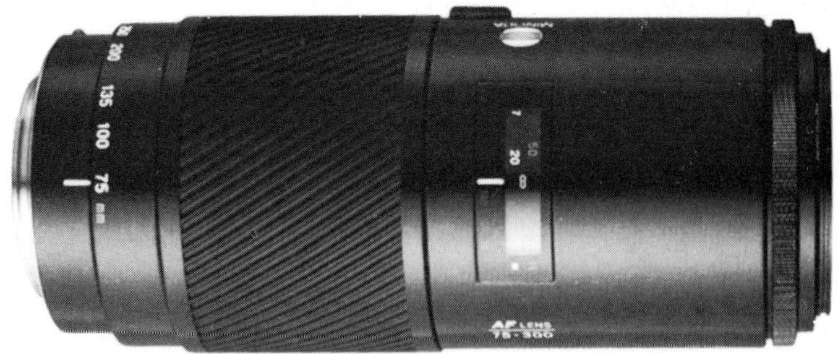
AF 75-300mm, f/4.5-5.6 zoom

weighing in at 1350g, with a price to match! It takes quite a commitment to first invest in, and then carry around, such a giant piece of optical engineering, but the benefits in reproduction quality cannot be disputed.

AF 100-200mm, f/4.5 zoom:
This is a relatively light and small AF zoom lens in the Minolta AF range. It weighs 375g and is 94.5mm in

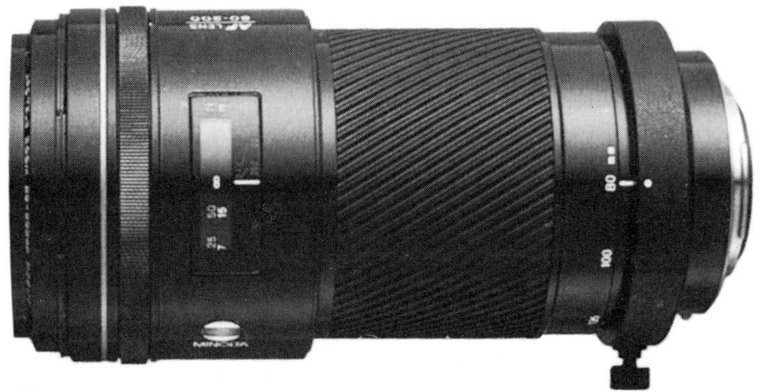

AF 80-200mm, 2.8 Apo zoom

length. Its special characteristic is the constant speed throughout the entire focal length range. Because of its light weight, compact construction, and acceptable price it makes an ideal partner for the 35-105mm or the 28-135mm AF zoom. Its filter diameter is 49mm. However, compared with the new Minolta 100-300mm AF zoom, it is not much smaller or lighter.

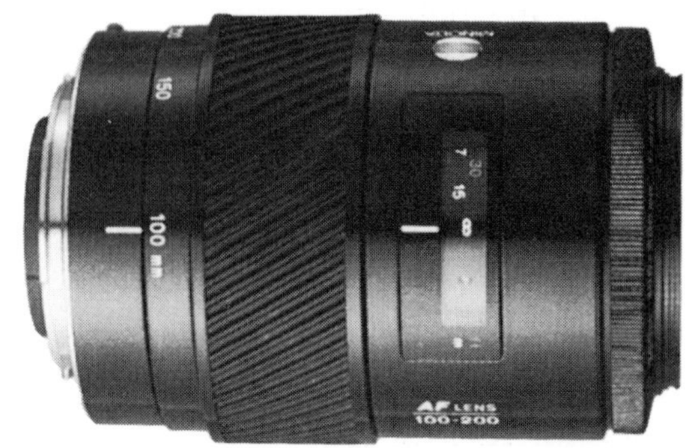

Af 100-200mm, f/4.5 zoom

Fixed Focal Lengths

AF Wide-Angle Lenses

AF 16mm,f/2.8 fisheye:
This lens possesses an extremely wide angle of view of 180° and fills the entire frame. Naturally, there is a price to pay for such an extreme angle of view: barrel-shaped distortion, i.e. the distortion of any straight lines that do not cross the centre of the frame. Its shortest focusing distance is 20cm. The peculiar perspective of this lens creates very unusual effects. However, extreme lenses such as this should be used sparingly, as one can very quickly get tired of the strange but quite characteristic interpretation of reality. Suitable subjects for the fisheye lens are landscapes and interiors. The lens hood is integrated, as is the revolving filter compartment with four integrated filters. The different filters can be moved into position by turning the holder. A further technical peculiarity of this lens is that the filters form an integral part of the lens construction, i.e. one of these filters always has to be in use. One is colourless, the others are orange (for black and white photography and infrared shots), pale pink (for

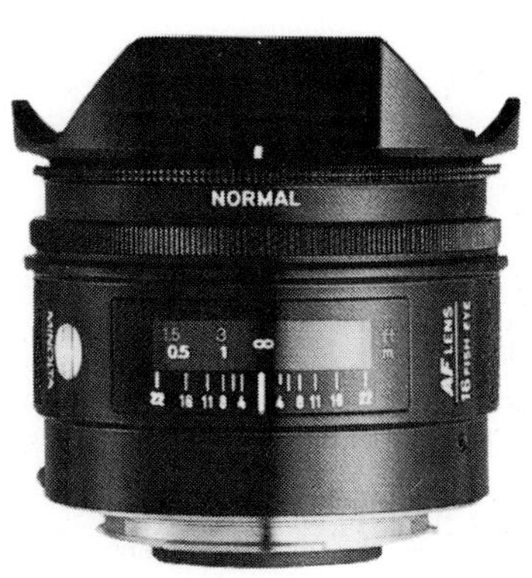

AF 16mm, f/2.8 Fisheye

colour photography under fluorescent lighting) and blue (for colour photography with tungsten lighting and daylight balanced film).

AF 20mm,f/2.8:

This extreme wide-angle lens has an angle of view of 94°. The large depth of field is particularly useful for architectural shots, landscape and action photography. Naturally, it is also very useful in restricted spaces such as interiors. Focusing is done by moving the rear elements only, thereby maximizing pre-

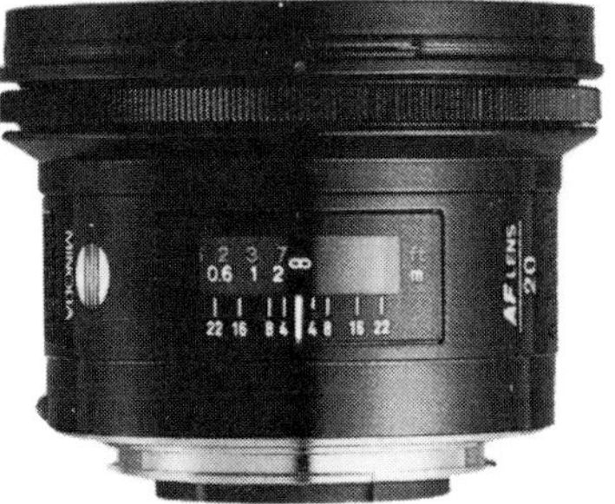

AF 20mm, f/2.8

cision and speed. The lens hood, which is supplied with the lens, can be inverted and kept on the lens for transport and storage purposes. The close-up limit is 25cm. This is a high quality lens of 10 elements arranged in 9 groups.

AF 24mm,f/2.8:

This lens also belongs to the group of super wide-angle lenses and possesses an angle of view of 84°. It is very compact and lightweight, particularly useful for action

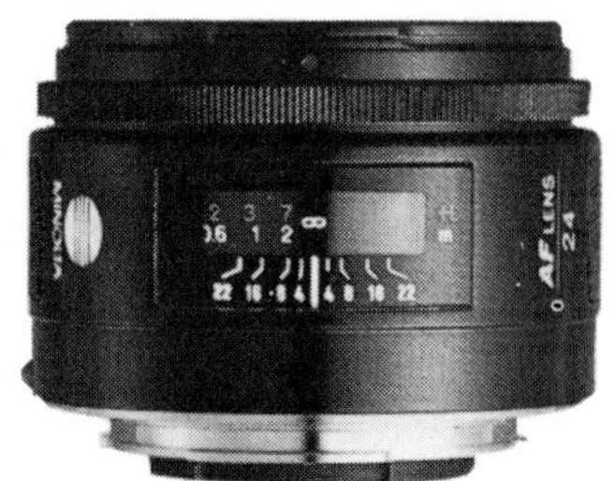

AF 24mm, f/2.8

photography and snap shots taken at close range. It is also ideally suited for landscape and architectural photography, and for interior shots in restricted spaces. The close-up limit is 25cm. It weighs 215g and as such is very handy for many photographic situations.

AF 28mm,f/2:

This lens comes into its own for wide-angle shots under poor lighting conditions, for example, landscapes in the dusk or poorly lit interiors. Its angle of view is a very considerable 75°. The optical construction of this extremely fast lens utilises 9 elements in 9 groups. The closest shooting distance is 30cm.

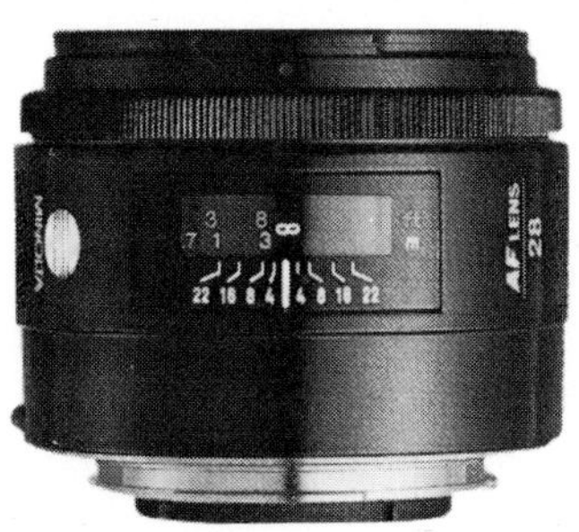

AF 28mm, f/2

AF 28mm,f/2.8:

This lens is one stop slower than the above lens but the advantage is that it is 100g lighter and 7mm shorter. The choice between this lens and the previous one lies between speed and weight. The travel photographer will probably choose the lighter lens, but if available-light photography is your par-

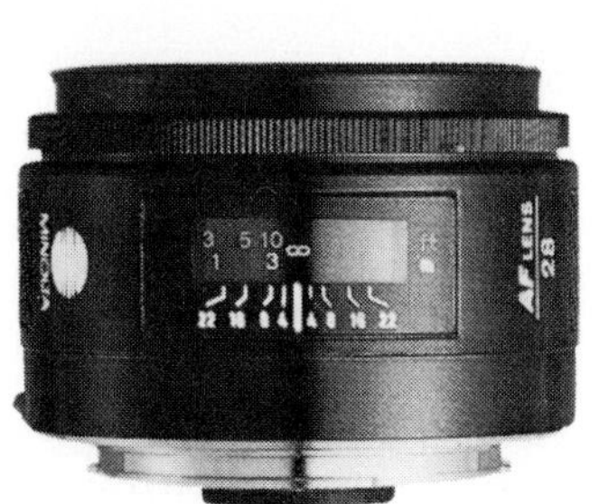

AF 28mm, f/2.8

ticular interest, then the faster f/2 lens will be the obvious choice. This lens weighs only 185g and is ideally suited for landscapes, interiors and snap shots at close range.

AF 35mm,f/1.4:

This extremely fast, moderately wide-angle lens, with a speed that is usually only offered with standard 50mm lenses, is useful as a universal lens for many applications. The moderate wide-angle is useful for moody landscapes at dusk or dawn, or for interiors in poor lighting without destroying the mood by using flash. The rather expensive construction with 10 elements arranged in 8 groups makes this a rather large and heavy lens. It weighs 470g and is, as such, the heaviest lens in the Minolta range of AF wide-angle lenses. Like the AF 85mm, f/1.4, this lens has a floating element, which improves the reproduction quality in the close range. Furthermore, it also has an aspherical element in the rear focusing section, which improves the lens quality and focusing time.

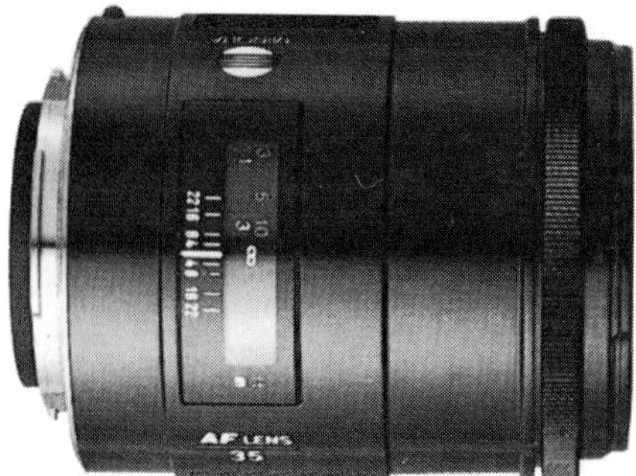

AF 35mm, f/1.4

AF 35mm,f/2:

Another excellent lens in this very useful focal length. This lens is one stop slower than the super fast 35mm,f/

1.4. If you are not specialising in extreme available-light situations, where it is necessary to work without flash in even the poorest lighting conditions, then this lens will serve you well. It weighs only 240g and boasts excellent reproduction qualities. For many photographers the weight of a lens is of great importance. In this case the choice is between this or one full stop extra at a price of twice the weight. The filter threads and close-up range are the same for both lenses, namely 55mm and 30cm.

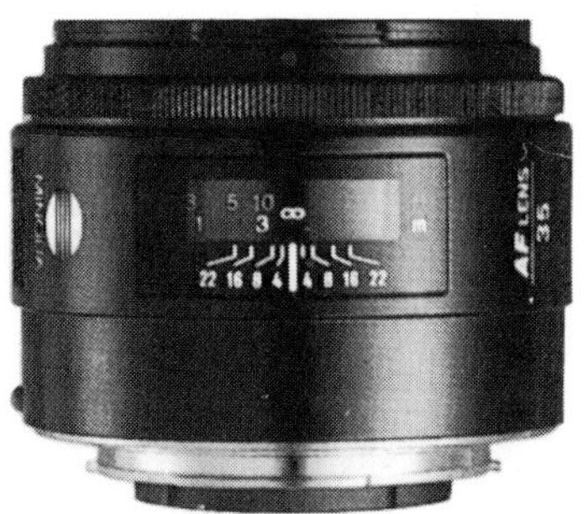

AF 35mm, f/2

Standard Lenses

AF 50mm,f/1.4:

In recent years standard lenses have declined in popularity. This is quite incomprehensible if one considers the great versatility, excellent quality and speed that usually accompanies a standard lens. Moreover, the angle of view of these lenses corresponds closely to that of the human eye, which lends pictures taken with them that particularly natural look. Some photographers may consider this boring, but the range of subjects that can be covered with the standard lens is practically unlimited. The great speed makes these lenses ideally suited for available-light photography. Conversely, the large aperture also allows great flash distances. It is a very fast example of this type of standard lens.

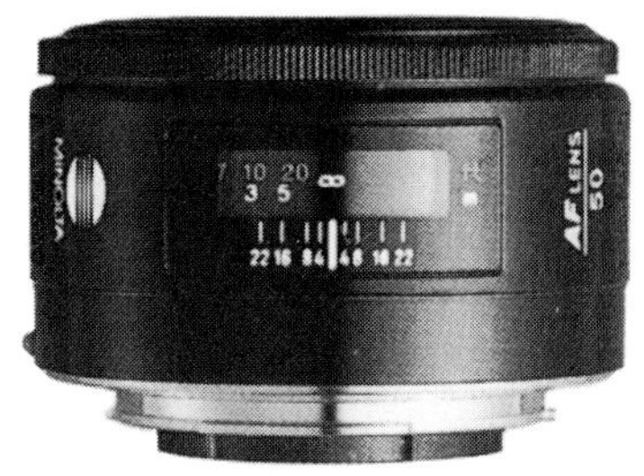

AF 50mm, f/1.4

AF 50mm,f/1.7:
This standard lens is still very fast. There are only three other lenses in the Minolta range of AF lenses that offer a faster speed. The dimensions of this lens are the same as its faster brother, but it weighs 50g less. The shortest close-up distance is 45cm, the same as that of the f/1.4. One considerable advantage of this lens, although it is half a stop slower, is its price. The argument in favour of standard lenses generally comprise their fast speed, lightness and excellent quality,

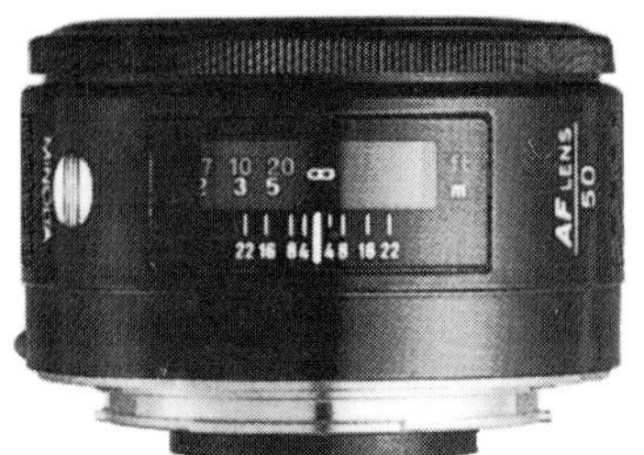

AF 50mm, f/1.7

all at a very reasonable price. The 50mm focal length is also covered in the Minolta programme by five AF zoom lenses.

Moderate Telephoto Lenses

AF 85mm,f/1.4:
This is a lens that is a particular favourite amongst professional photographers. Not surprisingly its exceedingly high speed facilitates shots in low level lighting, and a longer focal length provides precise control of the depth of field. This is particularly useful for portraits, where a blurred background is desirable.

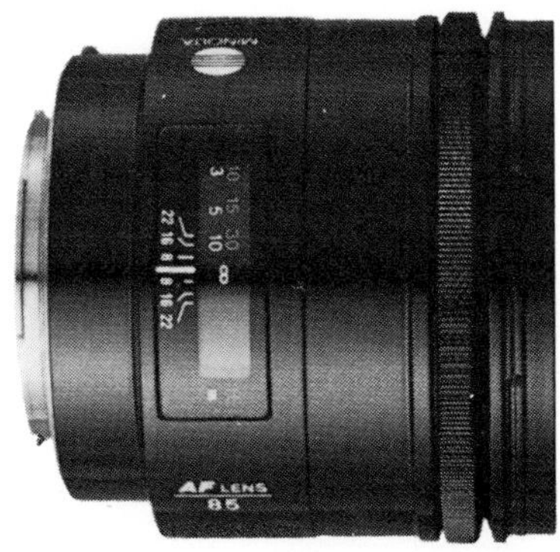

AF 85mm, f/1.4

Then there is the possibility of working in even poorer lighting conditions with relatively fast shutter speeds. The construction of this lens includes a floating element, which means that the groups of elements move in relation to each other during focusing.

AF 100mm,f/2:
The focal length of this lens is 15mm longer than the previous one but its overall length is only 4mm more; the speed is one stop less, but still a very powerful f/2. Its advantage over the 85mm lens, apart from the longer focal length, is that it is about 70g lighter. Furthermore, its filter diameter is only 55mm, 17mm less than the 85mm lens. In the choice between these

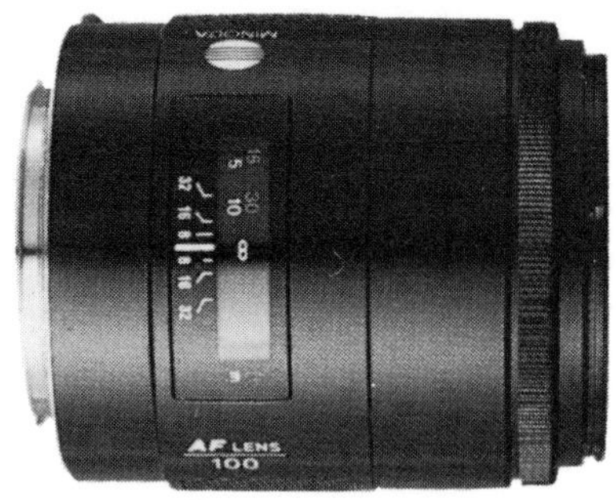

AF 100mm, f/2

two lenses the range of applications also has to be considered. In this case it will be a very personal choice. Both lenses are suitable for portrait photography and a decision will probably have to be made between a higher lens speed or a longer focal length and lighter weight. The price too will play an important role, but both of these lenses belong to the top range of Minolta AF lenses.

AF 135mm,f/2.8:
This is an excellent and more favourably-priced alternative to the 85mm and 100mm telephoto lenses described above. The lens speed is still a very respectable f/2.8, but its price is hardly more than a third that of the 85mm; it weighs 185g less and is only 11.5mm longer.

Moody evening scenes like these can be easily captured with centre-weighted average metering. The focal length of the lens will depend on how large the sun is to appear in the picture. ⇨

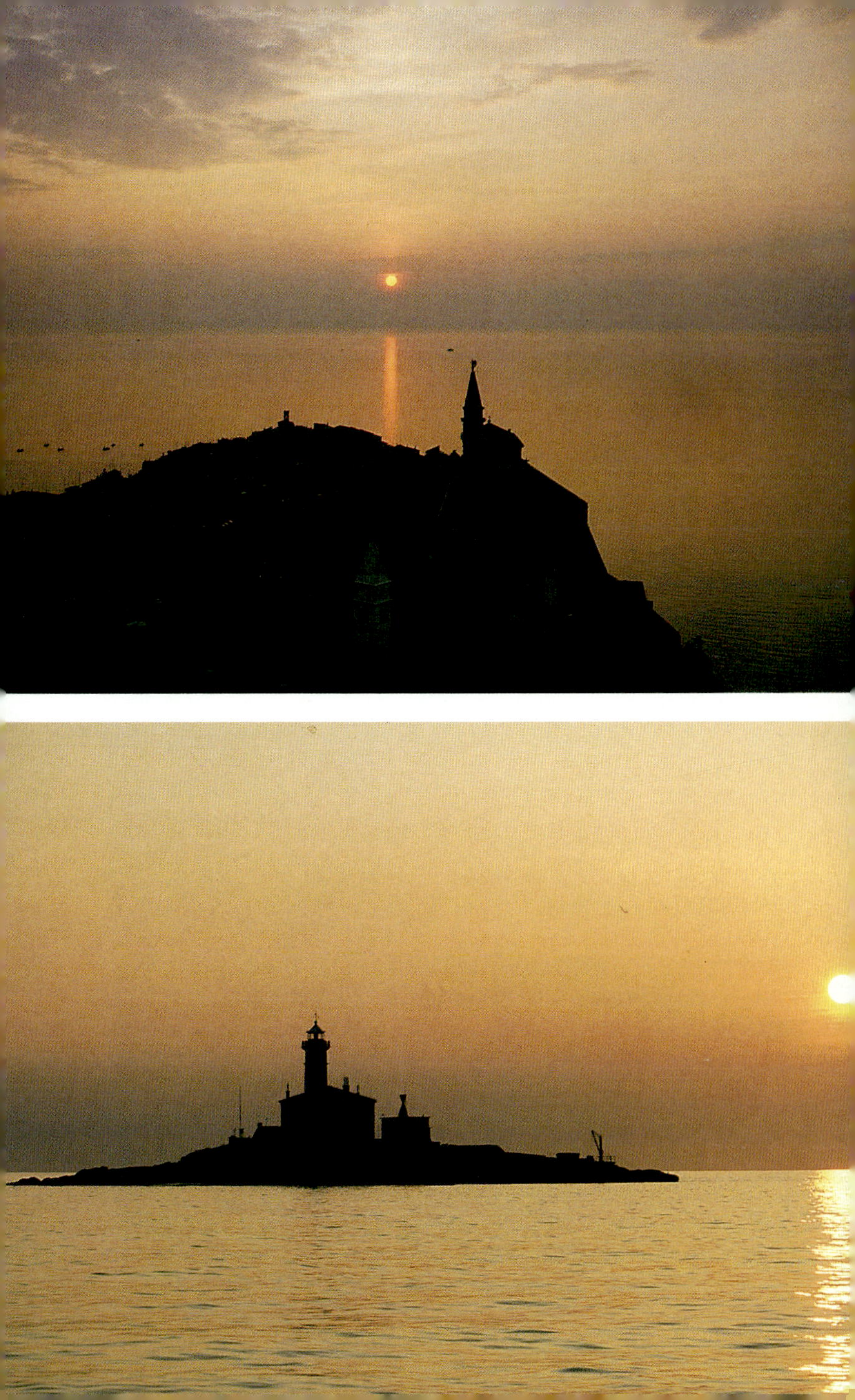

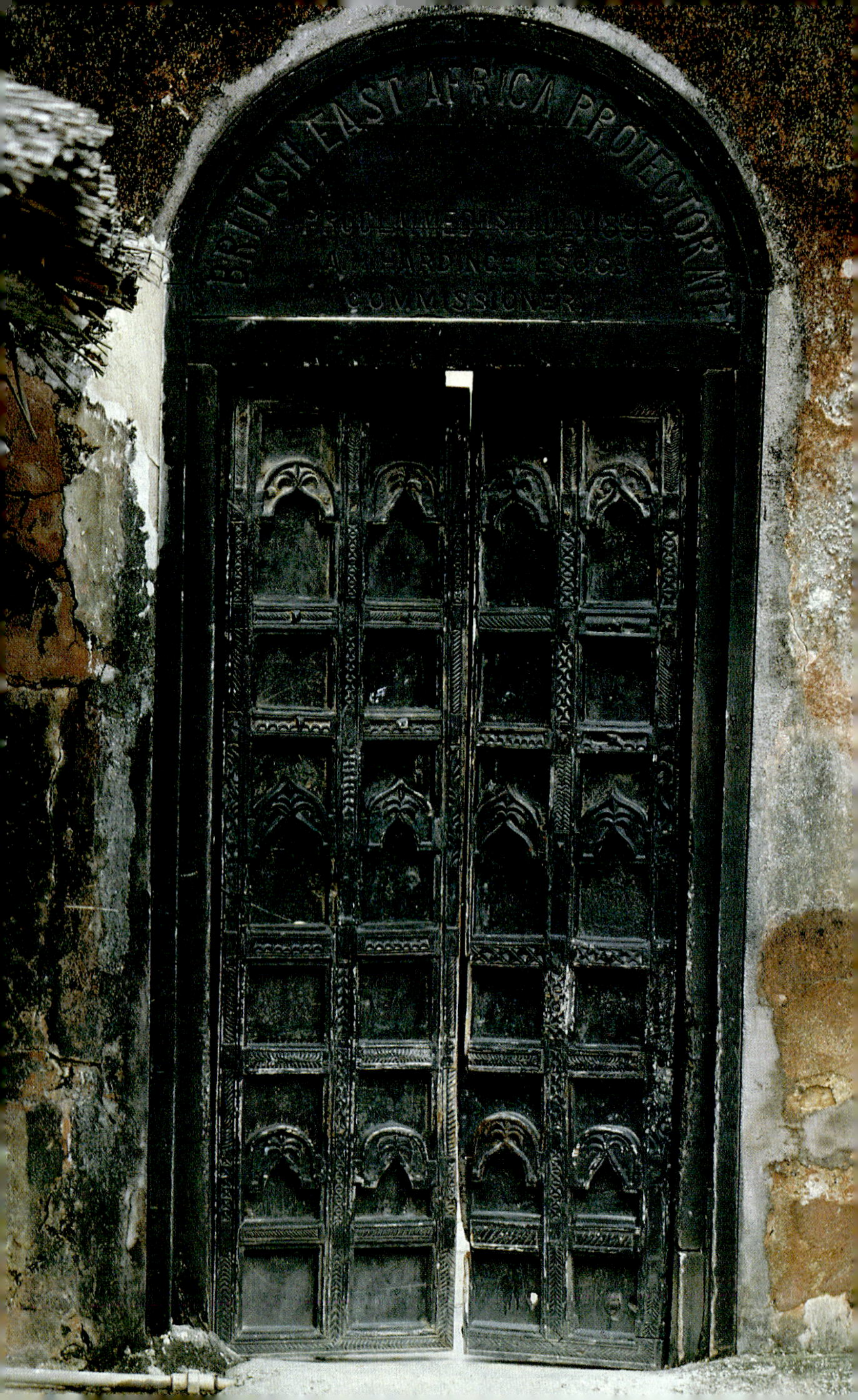
BRITISH EAST AFRICA PROTECTORATE
COMMISSIONER

This lens is also ideally suited for portrait photography, and, because of the extra focal length, it is very useful in sports and action photography. It has the same close-up distance of 1m and the resulting reproduction scale is therefore even greater than that of the 100mm lens with the same close-up distance.

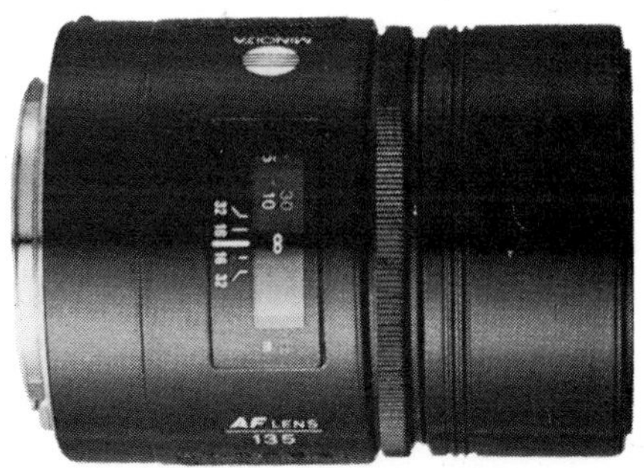

AF 135mm, f/2.8

Apochromatic Lenses

Apart from spherical aberration there is another reproduction error that causes problems for optical designers: chromatic aberration. In modern lenses spherical aberration is corrected, to a large extent, by the use of special aspherical elements. Chromatic

---

⇦ *Ornamental doors are a popular subject with most photographers. The dark texture of the wood is best reproduced by metering the lighter surrounding wall by the spot metering method and storing it while reframing the picture.*

aberration, on the other hand, is corrected by glasses with special refraction characteristics.

Chromatic aberration is a fault in colour representation, which manifests itself in fringes of different colours ringing objects in the image. This is due to unequal bending of the various colours of the spectrum as the light passes through the lens. This is because the amount of refraction is related to the wavelength of the light, which is different for different colours. Differences in the magnification and focusing of the different wavelengths result in overall fuzziness and colour fringes. This effect becomes particularly noticeable with longer focal lengths. Most lenses are constructed to correct only two of the spectral colours, which is generally quite satisfactory. This correction is obtained by the combination of several lenses, which cancel each other's defects. These types of lenses, with colour corrections for two colours, generally yellow and violet, are referred to as achromatic. The combination of positive and negative lenses of different types of glass is generally sufficient to achieve satisfactory correction.

A much better correction across the entire spectrum of blue, green and red is achieved by the so-called apochromatic lenses. Naturally, these are much more expensive as their optical construction necessitates the use of special glasses. Minolta use apochromatic lenses in some of their AF lenses; starting with the 200mm, as well as the AF 80-200mm,f/2.8 Apo. Especially for the Dynax generation of cameras Minolta developed the AF Apo 200mm, f/2.8, 300mm, f/2.8 and the 600mm, f/4; these lenses have been improved and equipped with a new ROM for faster focusing, and they also have a focus-stop button. The AF Apo Tele Converter II 2X and II 1.4X have also new control chips for

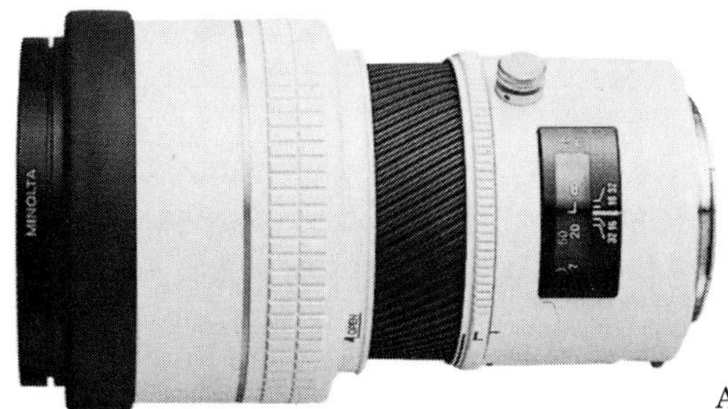

AF 200mm, f/2.8 Apo

faster communication with the camera. The installation of the new ROM-IC means that these Apo-Telephoto lenses will focus 1.5-times faster than the previous generation lenses. No changes have been made to the optical construction of these lenses.

AF 200mm,f/2.8 Apo:
This fast lens was constructed for the stringent demands of animal and sports photography. Automatic focusing is particularly fast and accurate by virtue of its internal focusing and pre-selection of the focusing range. Preselection of focusing range is effected by a special ring by which the largest or smallest focusing

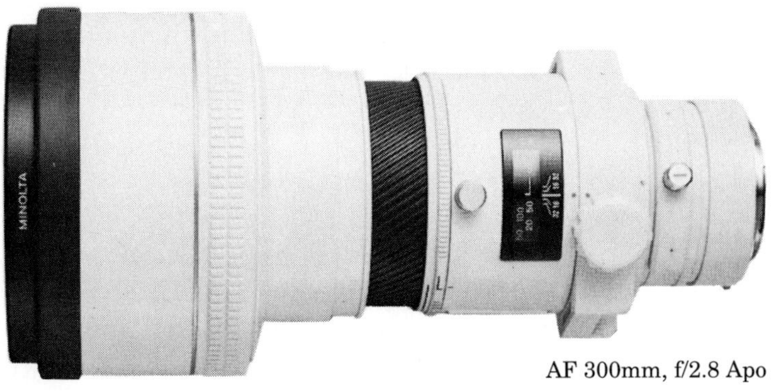

AF 300mm, f/2.8 Apo

distance is defined, preventing the auto-focus mechanism from having to traverse the whole focusing range. You may already know that the focusing movement required in the close range is relatively longer than for the far range. By limiting the close-up range to 5m, for example in sports photography, the focusing speed is doubled. The apochromatic correction is given by the use of two elements of AD glasses (AD = anomalous dispersion). This type of glass is sensitive to heat and the exterior colour of these lenses are white, instead of the usual black, to help reflect the sun's heat.

AF 300mm,f/2.8 Apo:
This is the most popular focal length for sports photography. Many sporting events take place in unevenly or poorly lit halls and as the action is usually fast, it is essential to use a wide aperture lens. Through the use of two AD elements, the AF 300mm,f/2.8 Apo, just like the shorter focal length 200m, has particularly good colour correction. It also has a focus range preselection ring so that the focusing range may be limited to either the close or far range. Internal focusing keeps the overall length of the lens constant by moving internal groups. The weight of nearly 3kg makes the use of a sturdy tripod an absolute must. As the weight of the lens could damage the camera bayonet, the lens itself

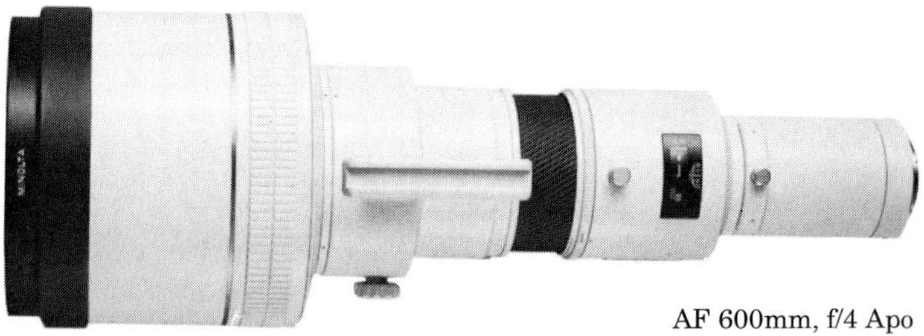

AF 600mm, f/4 Apo

has a tripod socket by which the lens and camera are supported in a balanced way. The lens may be turned in the tripod ring from horizontal to vertical format. A set of glass filters is also included. These are part of the optical construction and one filter always needs to be in place in the screw fitting of the filter holder. The set of filters comprises: colourless, yellow (Y-52), orange (O-56), red (R-60), neutral density (ND-4X), and skylight (1B). A12 (85) and B12 (80B) conversion filters are available separately.

AF 600mm,f/4 Apo:
A real heavyweight in every aspect. At over 5kg, it weighs nearly twice as much as the 300mm telephoto and is the longest lens in the Minolta programme but it is also the fastest of its kind. This lens will be used mainly by professional sports and animal photographers. Its price, which is beyond the pocket of ordinary photographers, (one could buy a small modern saloon car for the same money) will restrict this optical gem to the very few professionals who can justify such an investment. It goes without saying that nothing was spared in the construction of this lens. Apart from the special AD glasses, the front element is multi-coated to improve colour rendition and increase the contrast. Then there is internal focusing, focus range preselection and a tripod support ring as obviously hand-held shots are quite out of the question.

The precious front element is protected by a colourless filter which is supplied with the lens together with a similar set of filters as supplied with the 300mm. The lens has a sturdy handle for carrying and it is supplied in a case.

AF Apo Tele-Converters

Tele-Converters are very useful. They extend the focal length of a lens by a certain factor. Earlier Converters used to have the serious disadvantage that they degraded the reproduction quality but this has been overcome by reputable manufacturers. All converters reduce the speed of the lens but this is governed by optical laws and cannot be avoided. The Minolta AF Apo Converters have been designed as part of the total optical system with the lenses for which they are suitable. Like the lenses themselves they contain a ROM-IC which conveys to the camera all the necessary

AF 2x Teleconverter Apo
AF 1.4x Teleconverter Apo

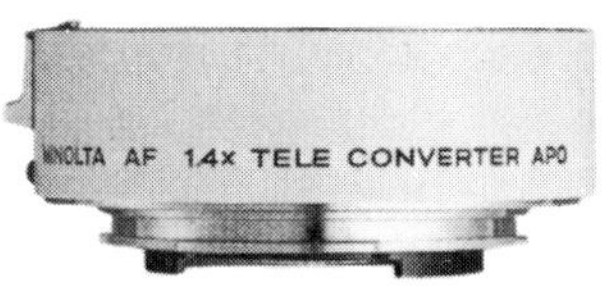

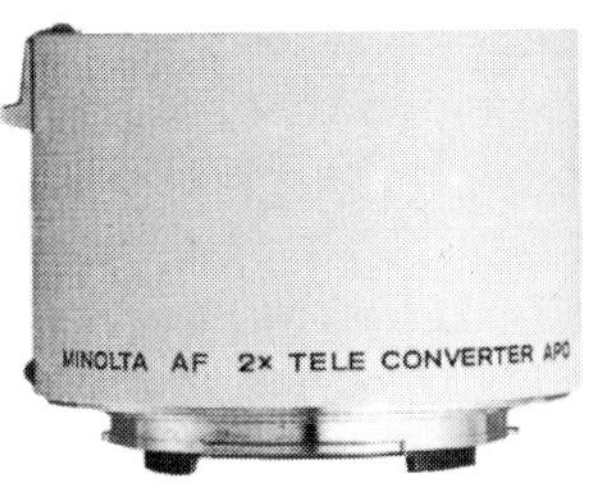

data, such as the actual aperture and focal length used at any given time. The data displayed in the viewfinder and the LCD panel are therefore correct and it is not necessary to take any correction factors into account. The computer-assisted design of the optical construction with special glasses and multi-coating guarantees excellent colour reproduction and good contrast even at full aperture. The autofocus function is not adversely affected either. A transmission mechanism in the Apo Tele-Converter combines the coupler with the camera, and the resulting focusing speed is only slightly slower than without the Converter. Minolta offers two Converters, one with a factor of 1.4x and the other of 2X.

AF 1.4X Tele Converter Apo:
This was specially designed for Minolta AF Apo lenses with focal lengths from 200mm. The use of this Converter extends the focal length of the original lens by a factor of 1.4. This means the 200mm becomes a 280mm lens, the 300m becomes a 420mm lens and the 600m becomes an 840mm lens. The lens speed of the original lens is reduced by one stop. As all Minolta AF Apo lenses have a very high speed, the loss in maximum aperture should present no real problem. The converters have the same colour finish as the AF Apo lenses and so form a harmonious unit with them.

AF 2X Tele-Converter Apo:
This doubles the focal length of a lens. It too was specially designed for Minolta AF lenses from 200mm. Using this Converter with the 200mm lens, converts it to a 400mm, with a 300m into a 600mm and with a 600m super-telephoto lens effectively you hold a 1200mm lens in your hand. One disadvantage of this converter is that the loss in speed of two stops is quite noticeable but this is still acceptable for many situations, due to the high speed of the Minolta AF Apo lenses.

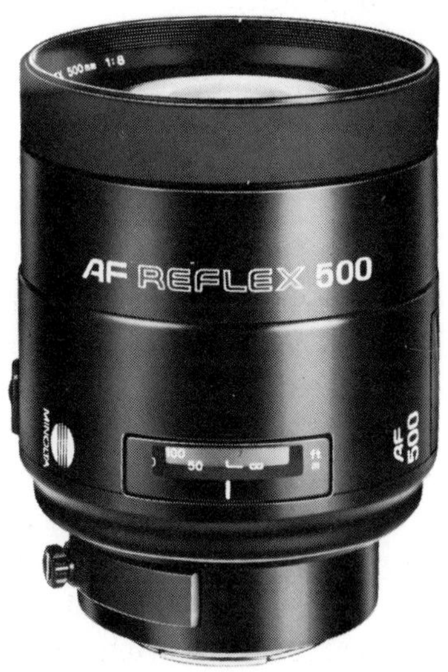

AF Reflex 500mm, f/8

The high optical quality of the Converter allows unrestricted use with full aperture. Its excellent qualities compensate to a certain degree for the loss in speed.

Minolta AF Reflex 500mm,f/8

This lens occupies a unique place among the Minolta AF lenses. This super-compact and very light telephoto lens has been specially developed for the Dynax generation of cameras and can be used with automatic and manual focusing on those cameras. Unfortunately it can only be focused manually with other Minolta AF cameras. The optical construction of this lens requires a slide-in filter in the tube, in front of the lens bayonet. The normal filter can be changed for the neutral density filter ND4x, which is supplied with the lens.

Optical construction: 7 elements in 5 groups, of which 2 are mirror lenses, and 1 filter. Close-up limit is approximately 4m. The aperture is fixed. Total weight 700g, length 118mm. It can be used with the Dynax 3000i but only with manual focusing.

AF Macro Lenses

Minolta offer two different focal length autofocus macro lenses, which are also perfectly suited for normal photography. The AF Macro Zoom 3X has been specially developed for reproduction ratios from 1:1 to 3:1. For copying or when you are working with relatively short shooting distances on a stand, it would be best to use the 50mm macro lens. For macro shots in the open, when you have to keep a certain distance from your subject, the 100mm macro lens would be better. Both

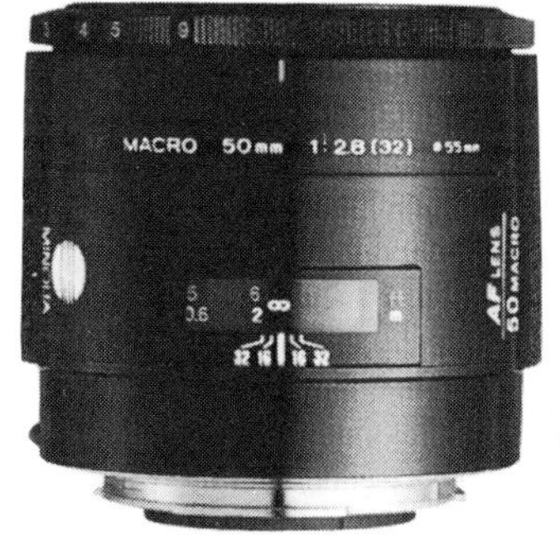

AF 50mm, f/2.8 Macro

lenses offer a reproduction ratio of 1:1, i.e. the subject is shown in the negative as life-size. The choice between one or the other lens will have to be decided by considering the potential applications against weight and price. If you are mainly interested in flowers, coins, etc., i.e. subjects that don't move, then the lower-priced 50mm would be your choice. If you are interested in small insects that cannot be approached too closely because you would scare them away, then you will have to dig deeper into your pocket and go for the 100mm macro. Otherwise they both offer the same reproduction scale of 1:1 and a speed of f/2.8. To illuminate the subject in the close range Minolta offer the Macro Flash 1200AF Set, which is attached by a special adapter ring to the filter thread of the macro lenses.

AF 50mm,f/2.8 Macro:
This lens can be focused continuously down to 1:1 and has a close-up limit of 20cm. Through the use of a double floating element system it was possible to compensate to a large extent for reproduction errors such as curvature of field and spherical aberrations. Three groups of elements move relative to each other during focusing, resulting in extremely rapid focusing. When the greatest reproduction scale is required the lens tube has to be extended to its maximum position, and this means that the distance between the subject and the front element is rather shorter than the quoted

AF 100mm, f/2.8
Macro

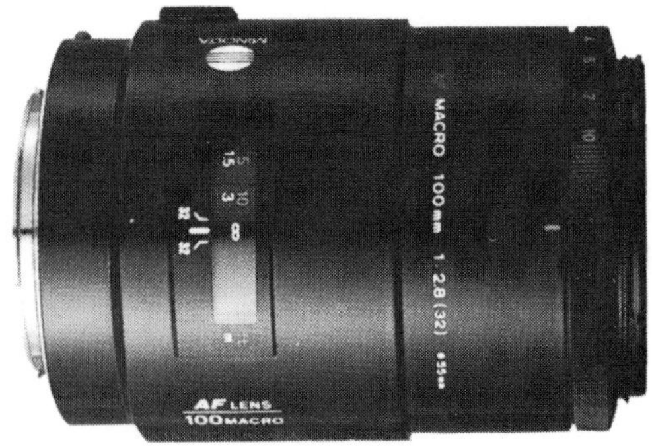

close-up distance of 20cm, which is defined as the distance between the subject and the film plane. This short distance also restricts the methods of illuminating the subject at this setting. Another important fact needs to be kept in mind: the greater the reproduction scale the smaller the depth of field. Minolta offer a Creative Expansion card for Macro Photography, which programs the camera for the special requirements of macro photography.

The exact reproduction scale may be read off from the position of the focusing ring. A ratio of 1:1 means the subject will be reproduced life size on the film; 1:2 means the subject will be shown half life size; and 1:1.5 means two-thirds life size. The sequence becomes easier to understand from 1:2 on, this means the reproduction scale is half life size. The sequence continues down to 1:9, which means the subject is shown nine times smaller in the negative than in its natural size.

AF 100mm,f/2.8 Macro:
With this macro lens the close-up distance, at full extension and reproduction scale of 1:1, is 15cm greater than that for the 50mm lens. This brings some very important advantages. First there are fewer problems in illuminating the subject. Secondly, a longer shooting distance to the subject is essential when shooting

small, shy creatures. The disadvantage is that this lens is considerably more expensive than the 50mm macro. The technically-advanced optical construction also embodies the double floating element system. There are eight freely moving elements, and three groups move simultaneously during focusing. By this special construction the lens tube can be kept relatively short. As with the AF telephoto Apo lenses, this macro lens has a distance range limiter to keep the focusing range to a certain limit, and so increase focusing speed. The close-up range can be limited to 54cm. For shooting at further distances the range is limited from 59cm to infinity.

Macro lenses are optimised for the close range but their reproduction quality in the far range is also extremely good and this is particularly true of the Minolta AF 100mm macro, which is also ideal for portrait photography.

AF Macro Zoom 3X-1X,f/1.7-2.8

This new and extremely fast Macro Zoom for special applications in the extreme close-up range has a limited reproduction ratio from 1:1 to 3:1; this means the size of the object on the negative is from life-size to three times its natural size.

Real Macro photography, i.e. when the reproduction ratio is large, is generally very difficult and cumbersome. This new lens handles some of the necessary settings automatically because the motor drives the opposed axial movements of the front mounting that carries the optical system and of the rear mounting that carries the camera housing. The middle mounting, which is normally fixed to a tripod, remains in a fixed position relative to the subject plane. The reproduction scale is continuously adjustable between 1:1

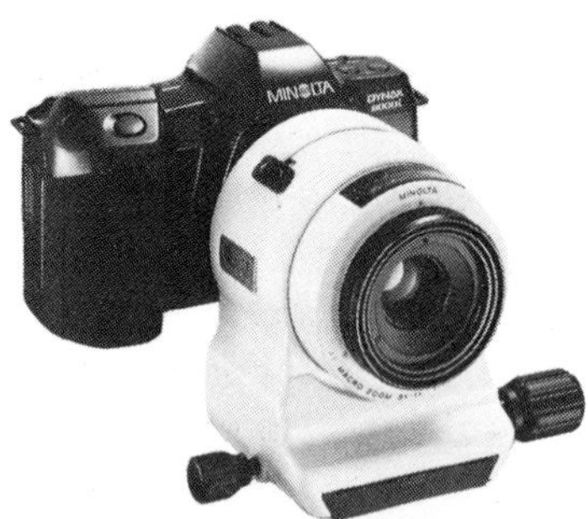

Minolta AF Macro Zoom 3x-1x, f/1.7-2.8
This is the very first AF macro lens in the world for reproduction ratios between 1:1 and 3:1 (life size to three-times life size).
The front and rear structual elements, carrying the camera housing and the optical system, move in opposite directions during focal length adjustment. The central focusing section, which can be mounted on a tripod, remains in a fixed position relative to the subject plane. A floating element system is employed to counteract aspherical and chromatic aberrations, which means that the distance between the two system components changes in relation to the reproduction ratio.

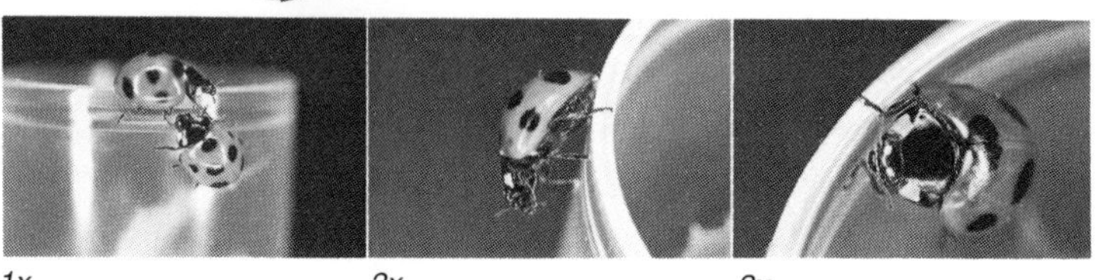

1x *2x* *3x*

and 3:1 and the value set at the time can be read off the scale on the lens.

After the required reproduction ratio is set, the automatic focusing functions are similar to that of a lens with internal focusing, i.e. the relative position between subject, lens and camera housing remains fixed. If desired it is also possible to use a knob to focus manually, whereby the lens and the camera move together on a focusing track.

To reduce spherical and chromatic aberrations the lens utilizes a floating element. The close-up distances of the lens are between 25.1 mm (at 3:1) to 40.1 mm (at 1:1).

This lens can be used with the Dynax 8000i either with one of the automatic shooting modes or in manual shooting mode. If one of the automatic shooting modes is used, the camera will automatically compensate for the loss of light that is experienced with these large reproduction ratios;

in this case no compensation factors have to be calculated and added to the camera's automatic settings.

The motorized setting of the framing is another unique feature of this lens. It is often very difficult to adjust the framing when taking subjects so close up. On the base of the lens is a slide switch which allows the camera housing to be moved quite easily to achieve the desired framing. The lens may be turned through 135°. The filter thread measures 46mm. This is the same switch as is used for altering the magnification. Its function is changed by a selector switch on top of the lens barrel.

The zoom motor and camera movements are powered by a 6v lithium battery, which is accommodated in the lens mount.

You will not be surprised to hear that all these features, particularly the high speed, have to be bought at quite a high price which removes this lens from the reach of the ordinary amateur photographer. It is supplied together with a very special macro tripod that allows the lens/camera unit to be moved over the subject, similar to the way a microscope is operated.

The special Macro Flash 1200AF Set can be mounted to the front of the lens for flash photography. However, it has to be considered that the autofocus will not function if the modelling lights are used on a subject with insufficient contrast.

The lens speed varies with changing reproduction ratio, but it is not too difficult to ascertain the exact lighting by using a hand-held exposure meter. Contrary to conventional bellows, the aperture value displayed in the viewfinder or on the data panel is the actual effective aperture and there is no need to make any exposure adjustment to compensate for magnification.

This expensive marvel is supplied with covers for both the front and rear element, a hard case and macro tripod.

The Minolta AF Lens Range

Lens	Elements/ Groups	Angle of view	Closet focusing distance	Smalltest aperture	Filter diameter	Dimensions	Weight
AF-Fisheye 2,8/16 mm	11/8	180°	0,2 m	22	integr.	75 x 66,5 mm	400 g
AF 2,8/20 mm	10/9	94°	0,25 m	22	72 mm	77,5 x 53,5 mm	285 g
AF 2,8/24 mm	8/8	84°	0,25 m	22	55 mm	65,5 x 44 mm	215 g
AF 2/28 mm	9/9	75°	0,3 m	22	55 mm	66,5 x 49,5 mm	285 g
AF 2,8/28 mm	5/5	75°	0,3 m	22	49 mm	65,5 x 42,5m	185 g
AF 1,4/35 mm	10/8	63°	0,3 m	22	55 mm	65,5 x 76 mm	470 g
AF 2/35 mm	7/6	63°	0,3 m	22	55 mm	66,5 x 48,5 mm	240 g
AF 1,4/50 mm	7/6	47°	0,45 m	22	49 mm	65,5 x 38,5 mm	235 g
AF 1,7/50 mm	6/5	47°	0,45 m	22	49 mm	65,5 x 38,5 mm	185 g
AF 1,4/85 mm	7/6	28°30′	0,85 m	22	72 mm	78 x 71,5 mm	550 g
AF 2/100 mm	7/6	24°	1,0 m	32	55 mm	67 x 75,5 mm	480 g
AF 2,8/135 mm	7/5	18°	1,0 m	32	55 mm	65,5 x 83 mm	365 g
AF-Apo 2,8/200 mm	8/7	12°30′	1,5 m	32	72 mm	86 x 134 mm	790 g
AF-Apo 2,8/300 mm	11/9	8°10′	2,5 m	32	integr.	128 x 238,5 mm	2480 g
AF-Apo 4/600 mm	10/9	4°10′	6,0 m	32	integr.	169 x 449 mm	5500 g
AF-Reflex 8/500 mm*	7/5	5°	4,0 m	–	integr.	89 x 118 mm	665 g
AF 4/24-50 mm	7/7	84°-47°	0,35 m	22	55 mm	69 x 60 mm	285 g
AF 3,5-4,5/28-85 mm	13/10	75°-29°	0,8 m	22-27	55 mm	68,5 x 85,5 mm	490 g
AF 4-4,5/28-135 mm	16/13	75°-18°	1,5 m	22-27	72 mm.	75 x 109 mm	750 g
AF 4-5,6/35-80 mm	8/8	63°-30°	0,5 m	22-32	46 mm	65 x 58 mm	195 g
AF 3,5-4,5/35-105 mm	12/10	63°-23°	0,85 m	22-27	55 mm	68,5 x 59,5 mm	290 g
AF 3,5-4,5/70-210 mm	12/12	34°-12°	1,1 m	22-27	55 mm	72,5 x 163,5 mm	420 g
AF 4,5-5,6/75-300 mm	13/11	32°-8°10′	1,5 m	32-38	55 mm	72,5 x 163,5 mm	865 g
AF-Apo-Zoom 2,8/80-200 mm	16/13	30°-12°30′	1,8 m	32	72 mm	87,5 x 166,5 mm	1350 g
AF-Zoom 4,5-5,6/80-200 mm	9/9	30°-12°30′	1,5 m	22-27	46 mm	67 x 78 mm	290 g
AF-Zoom 4,5/100-200 mm	8/7	24°-12°30′	1,9 m	22	49 mm	69,5 x 94,5 mm	375 g
AF-Zoom 4,5-5,6/100-300 mm	11/9	24°-8°10′	1,5 m	32-38	55 mm	72,5 x 100 mm	410 g
AF-Macro 2,8/50 mm	7/6	47°	0,2 m	32	55 mm	68,5 x 59,5 mm	310 g
AF-Macro 2,8/100 mm	8/8	24°	0,35 m	32	55 mm	71 x 98,5 mm	520 g
AF-Macro-Zoom 3X-1X (1:1,7-1:2,8)	7/5	24 x 36 mm (1x)** 8 x 12 mm (3x)**	40 mm (1x) 27 (1x) 25 mm (3x) 16 (3x)	27 (1x) 16 (3x)	46 mm	86 x 117 x 94,5 mm***	1100 g
AF-Apo-Telekonverter II 1,4X	5/4	–	–	–	–	64 x 20 mm	175 g
AF-Apo-Telekonverter II 2X	6/5	–	–	–	–	64,5 x 43,5 mm	210 g

Focal length ranges of Minolta AF-zoom lenses

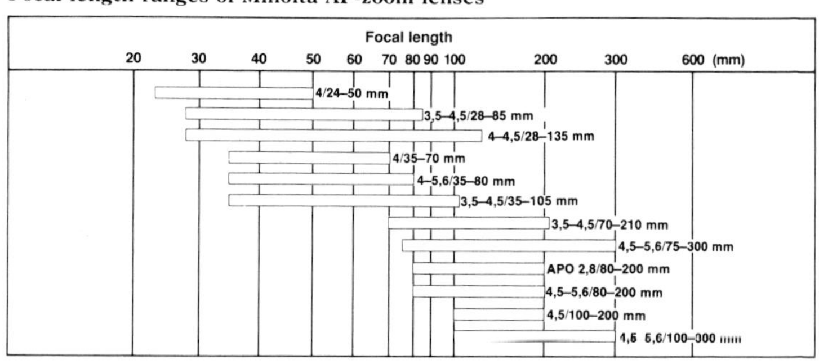

The Expansion Card System

The Minolta Dynax 8000i is the third camera in the Dynax generation that can be programmed by Creative Expansion cards to extend and modify its basic function modes. There are now 13 of these cards available which can be used in special shooting situations or with special equipment. They can be roughly divided into three groups. The Customized Function card occupies a special position; this card is used for programming or reprogramming individual camera functions and it forms a group on its own. The second group are eight feature cards for function extensions and the third group are the four special application cards.

When the card is activated, data flow between the micro processor of the card and the camera computer is initiated. Depending on the programming of the card, the micro processor influences the autofocus function, exposure and film transport. The cards are inserted into the card door which is built into the hand grip. As soon as a card is inserted, its function is automatically activated and the word **CARD** appears in the data panel. The name of the card is displayed for about five seconds in the top line of the data panel. If it is the Customized Function card, or certain Feature cards, then it is necessary to press the **CARD-ADJ** button, which is located inside the card door, in order to adjust the functions. No manual setting is necessary for the Special Application Cards.

Programming of the required functions is simple.

The selected special functions can be cancelled at any time. To temporarily return to normal operation, just press the **CARD** on/off key, situated by the data panel and this resets the camera to basic functions. For most cards the functions initiated are retained only as long as the card remains inserted. The Customized Function card is the exception. The functions selected with this card remain in memory, even after the card has been removed.

Customized Function Card

There are a total of seven camera functions that can be programmed individually to the requirements of the photographer.

1.Choice of exposure mode:
Not every photographer needs all the exposure programs that are offered by the Dynax 8000i. Using this card, the photographer can deactivate any exposure modes that he does not intend to use. This has the advantage that he can change very quickly from one function to another without having to step through unwanted exposure modes. The preparatory actions and settings needed in picture taking can thus be streamlined. The photographer can choose freely which exposure modes he wishes to retain, if he wants more than one, and which combination of functions would suit him best. The program mode will always be retained, and any of the other exposure modes, i.e. aperture priority **A,** shutter speed priority **S** or manual exposure mode **M,** can be selected to remain active individually or collectively. There is a total of eight combinations available.

To change the camera functions: Open the flap of the hand grip, insert the card in the slot, and press the **CARD-ADJ** button. In the data panel **CARD** and the present functions and settings will flash. This indicates that you are now able to make your another selection and the release button and autofocus function are inactive. Press the **CARD** on/off key to select function 1; **CUSt-1** will appear in the LCD panel, now you can choose one of the eight combinations by moving the setting control. This is stored by again pressing the **CARD-ADJ** button.

2.Focus-Stop Button:

The two new Minolta AF zoom lenses, the 70-210mm and the 100-300mm, have a button by which the focus process can be stopped. This button can be reprogrammed to select the centre focus area or continuous autofocus. Press the **CARD** on/off key to select function 2, which is displayed as **CUSt-2,** then use the setting control to select an option - **1** for focus hold; **2** for centre focus area; and **3** for continuing autofocus.

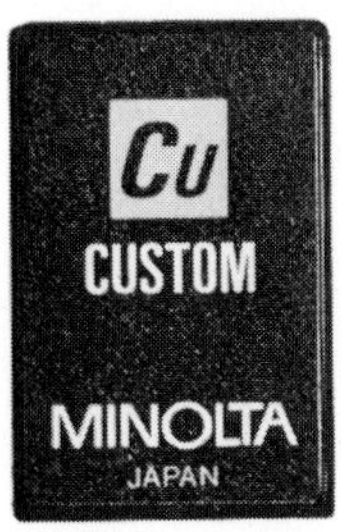

Modifications possible with the Customized Function Card:

❍ Selectable exposure modes: P, A, S, or M; P, A, or M; P, A, or S; P, or A; P, S, or M; P or M, P or S; P.
❍ Shutter speed: adjustable in half or full stops
❍ Audible signal: not applicable with Dynax 8000i
❍ Frame counter: in ascending or descending order
❍ Film rewind: automatic or manual
❍ Film leader: rewound into cassette or left out
❍ Focus-hold button: focus hold, centre area focus, or continuous focus adjustment.

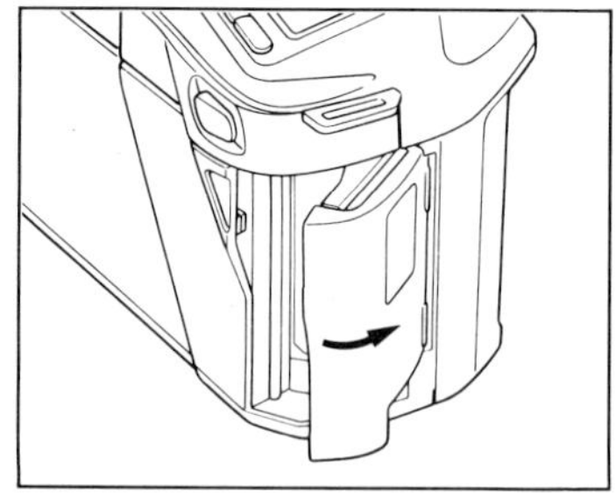

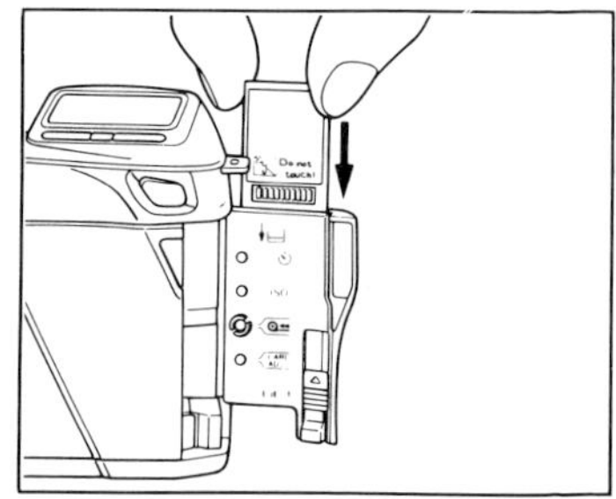

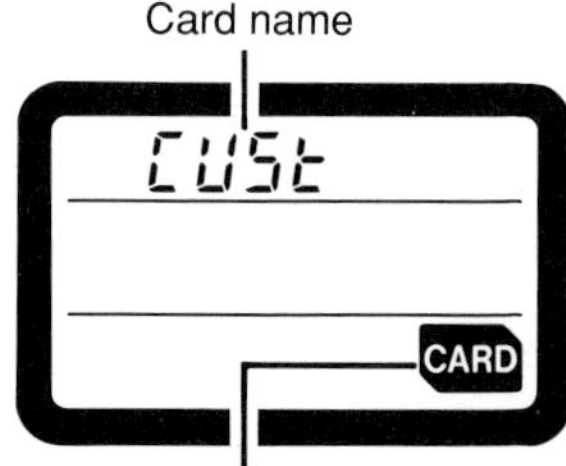

Insert card into camera:

1. set main switch to ON or •))).
2. open card door
3. insert card into slot with contacts pointing inward.

In the data panel the top display appears. After five seconds it reverts to normal.

If the display is not as shown, check if the card has been properly inserted.

To remove the card, push card-eject slide up.

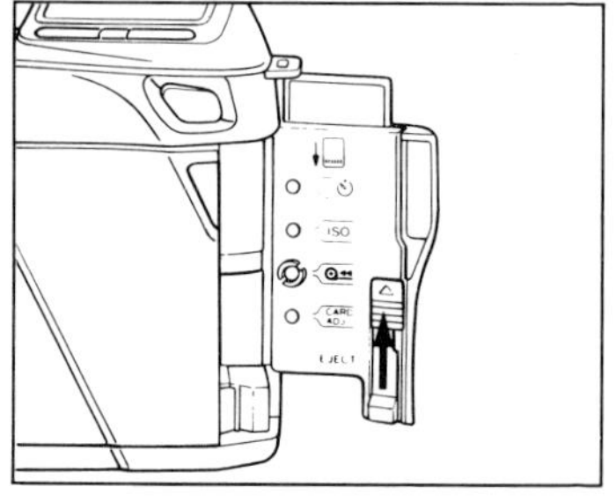

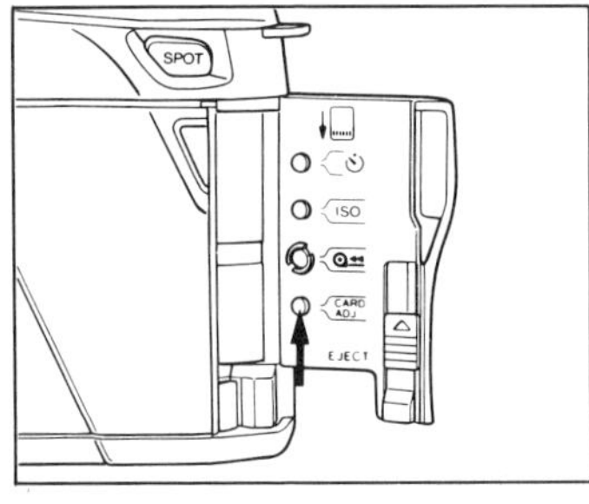

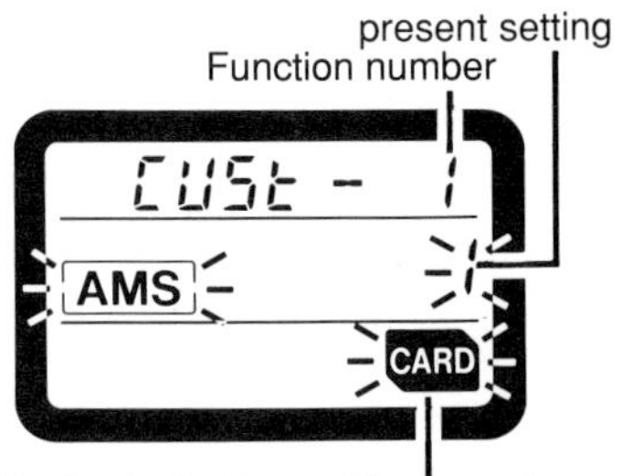

Display indicating settings can be adjusted

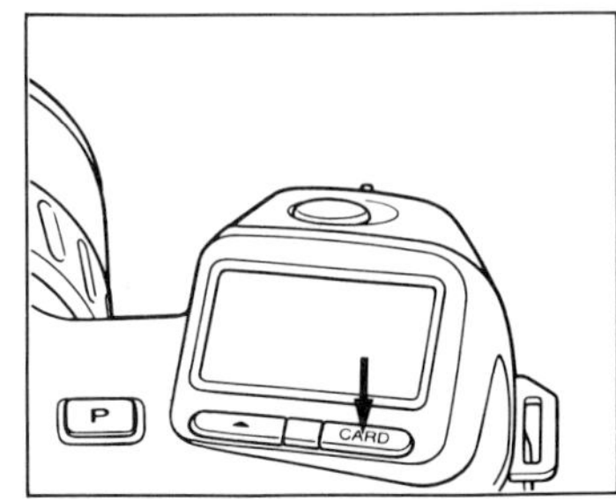

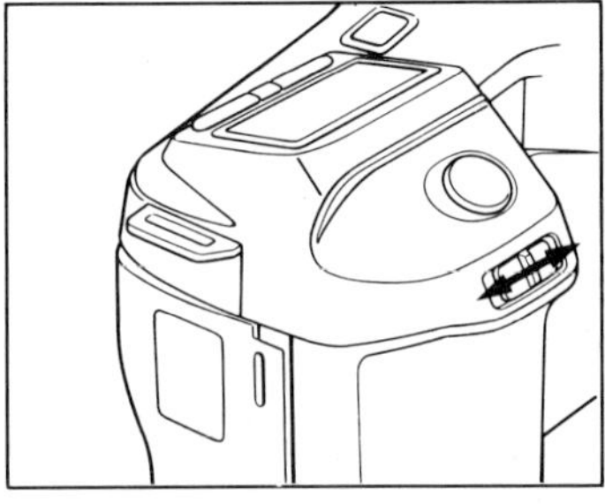

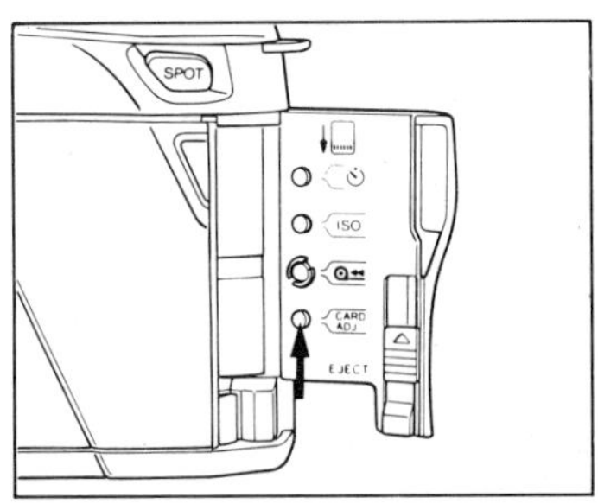

Changing the settings:

With main switch to ON and card inserted, proceed as follows:

1. The display for the inserted card, the function number and the present setting will be displayed in the data panel. Open card door and press card-adj button. The display flashes to indicate settings can be changed. Neither autofocus or shutter release function will function.
2. Press CARD On/off key to change the function number.
3. Select the required value by setting control.
4. Repeat steps in 2 and 3 each time you wish to change function and setting values.
5. After everything is set, press the card adj button again. This will store the selected settings in memory even if the card is removed.

3.Shutter Speed Settings:
Manual shutter speed preselection in shutter speed priority or in manual is effected in one stop increments. The card allows the photographer to choose between half and full stop increments. Press the **CARD** on/off key when **CARD** flashes in the LCD panel, and select function 3, displayed as **CUSt-3,** then use the setting control to choose between setting **1** for whole stops and setting **2** for half stops, the setting numbers being displayed in the second line of the data panel.

4. Audible Warning for Slow Shutter Speeds:
This function is not used with the Dynax 8000i as it does not emit an audible warning signal.

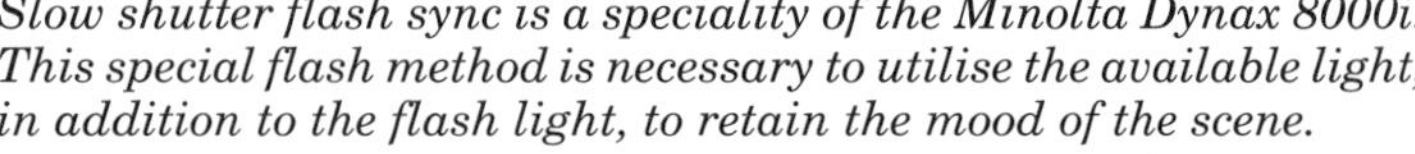

Slow shutter flash sync is a speciality of the Minolta Dynax 8000i. This special flash method is necessary to utilise the available light, in addition to the flash light, to retain the mood of the scene. ⇨

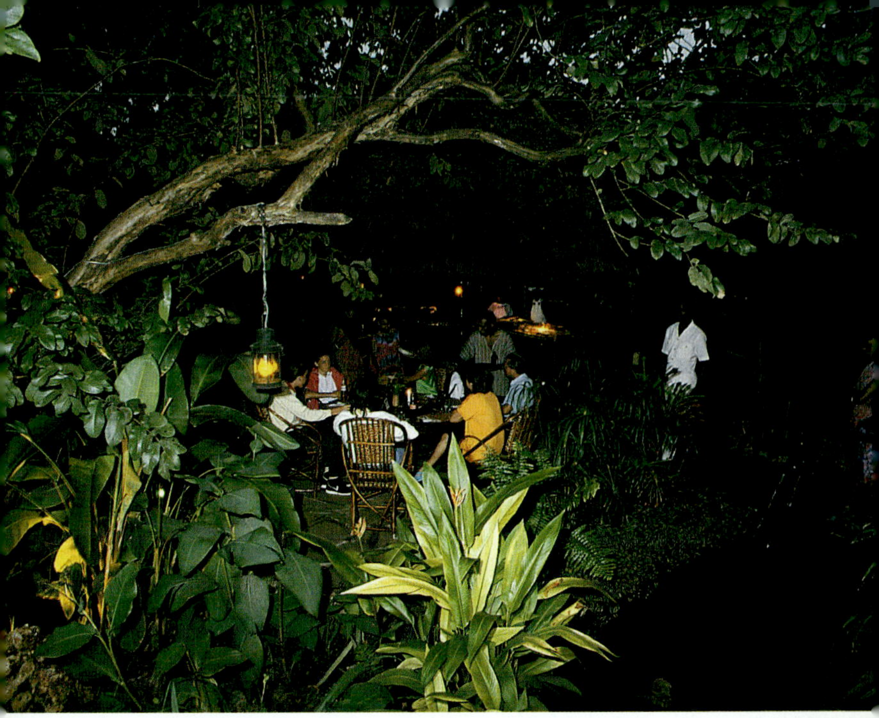

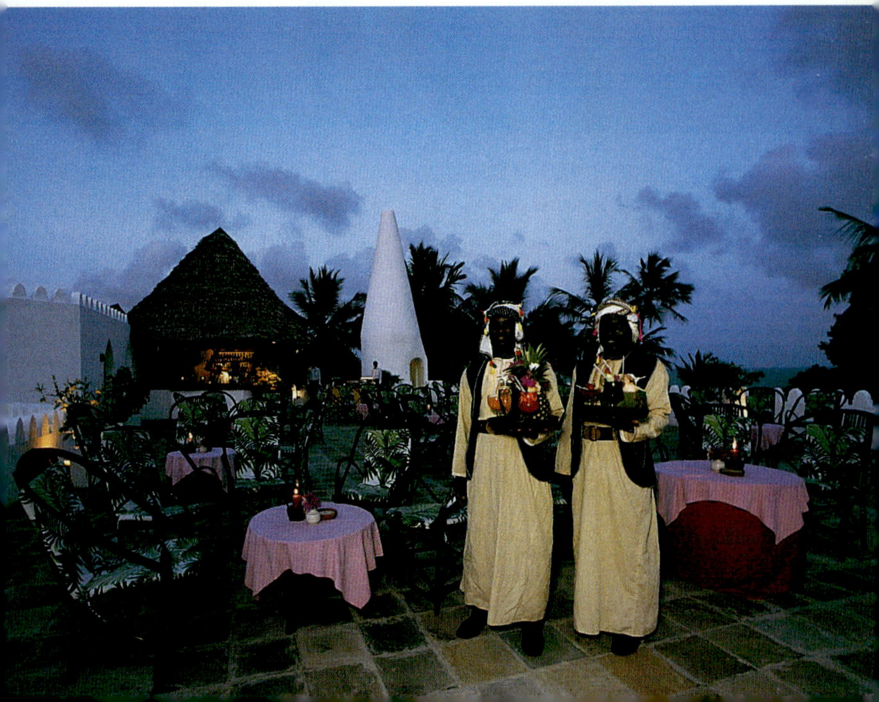

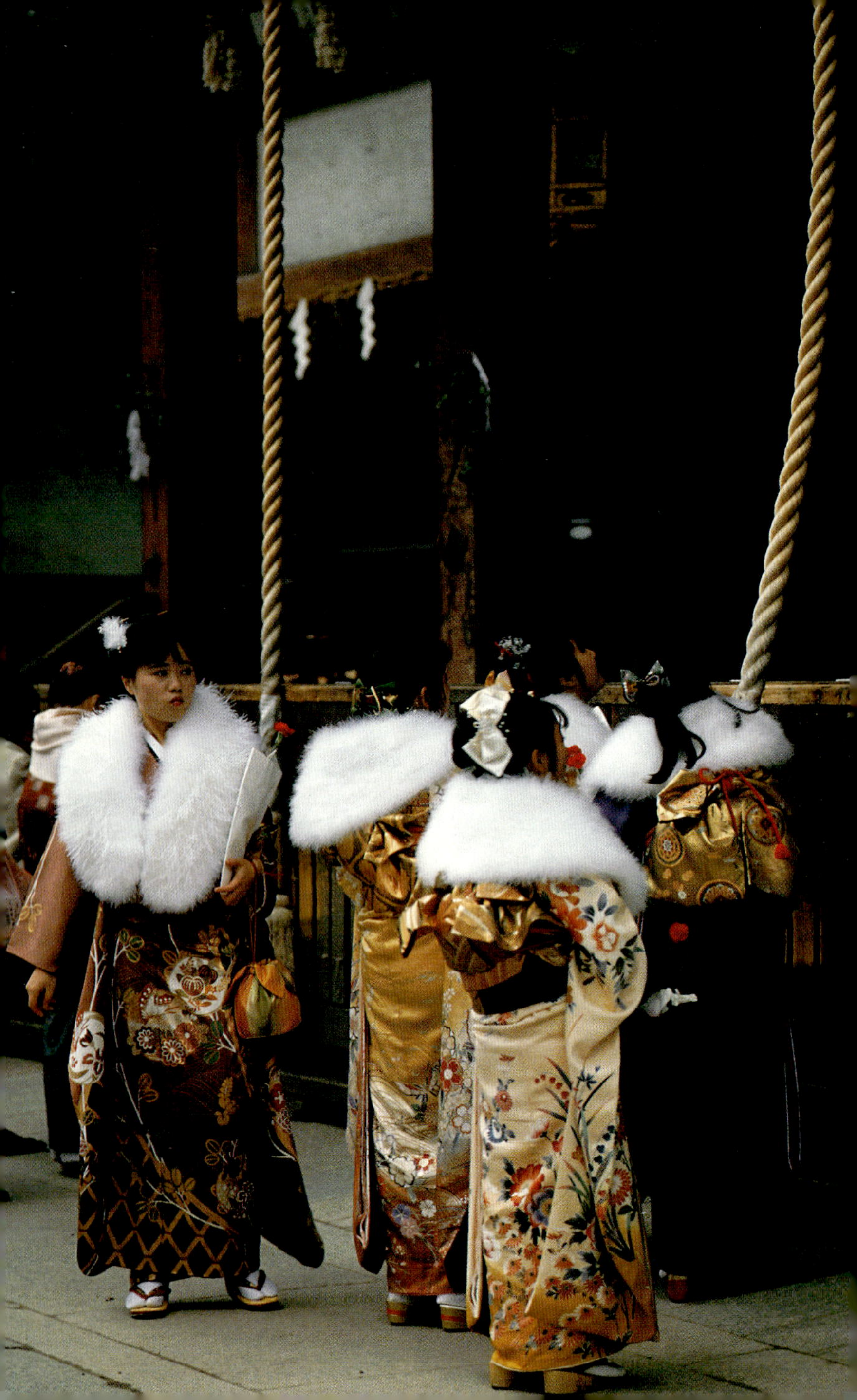

5.Frame Counter:

The frame counter in the Dynax 8000i counts the number of exposed frames. This function can be reprogrammed so that the camera displays the number of unexposed frames remaining. Choose function number 5, displayed as **CUSt-5** when **CARD** flashes and press the **CARD** on/off key. By moving the setting control select either **1** for forward counting, or **2** for counting down the remaining frames. This function is possible because the Dynax 8000i is able to recognize not only the film speed of the loaded film, but also the number of exposures by reading this information off the coding on the cassette. With a film that is not DX-coded, the counter will always count forward.

⇦ *AF-integrated multi-pattern metering is particularly suitable for subjects with large illumination contrasts.*

6.Film Rewinding:

As soon as the last exposure is made the Minolta Dynax 8000i will automatically rewind the film into the cassette. In some situations this could be inconvenient; for example the noise of the motor may disturb shy creatures. Using this card you can reprogram the camera not to rewind the film automatically. Press the **CARD** on/off key when **CARD** flashes in the data panel and select function 6, displayed as **CUSt-6.** The choice is between setting **1** for automatic rewinding and setting **2** for manual rewind start. If the latter is chosen then you have to press the rewind button in the card door to initiate motorised rewinding.

7.Film Leader:

It is a matter of personal taste whether it is better to rewind an exposed film entirely into the cassette or to allow the film leader to protrude. The Dynax 8000i is programmed to completely rewind the film into the cassette as this prevents reloading an already exposed film. This card lets the photographer reprogram the camera to allow the film leader to protrude from the camera which makes it easier to remove the film from the cassette for processing. To choose this option, select function number 7, displayed as **CUSt-7** in the data panel, and use the setting control to select either setting **1** for complete rewinding or setting **2** to leave the film leader protruding.

The first setting in all the function options is always 1. This corresponds to the basic programming of the Dynax 8000i and can always be kept, or modified, as required. As soon as all modifications are completed, the settings are stored by pressing the **CARD-ADJ** button in the card door. Once set, these options are retained, even if the card is removed from the camera. The functions modification cannot be temporarily changed by pressing the **CARD** on/off key. The Customized Function card is the only card that can be used in this way, and can also be combined with other cards. After removing the Customized Function card you can insert another card, using the **CARD** on/off key. These additional card functions may now be activated and deactivated. If **CARD** is displayed in the data panel, then the additional functions of the inserted card are activated, otherwise the camera will work with the settings that have been previously stored.

Function number	Function	Setting number	Remark
1	Selectable exposure modes	1	P (Program mode), A (Aperture priority mode), S (Shutter speed priority mode) or M (manual function).
		2	P, A or M
		3	P, A or S
		4	P or A
		5	P, S or M
		6	P or M
		7	P or S
		8	P
2	AF focus-hold (AF 70-210mm and 100-300mm Zoom lenses)	1	Focus-hold
		2	Centre Focus Area
		3	Continuous Autofocus
3	Shutter speeds (exposure modes M and S)	1	Full exposure stop
		2	Half exposure stop
4	Not applicable with Dynax 8000i		
5	Frame counter	1	Normal (increasing) counting
		2	Backwards (decreasing)
6	Film rewind	1	Automatic
		2	Manual
7	Film leader	1	Entirely rewound into cassette
		2	Leader protruding

Default value of all settings is 1.

Feature Cards

There are several cards now available in this group. They allow the extension of various camera functions and render the Minolta Dynax 8000i even more versatile than it already is. They are for automatic exposure bracketing, program shift, and assessment of highlight and shadow spot metering, for multiple spot metering, multiple exposures, bracketing of flash exposures, storage of exposure data, and for the creation of special effects.

Exposure Bracketing Card

Correct exposure is not always just a question of proper metering; you may wish to vary it within certain limits for different films, and finally and most importantly it is a question of personal taste. The colour rendering of slide films, in particular, is often better if they are

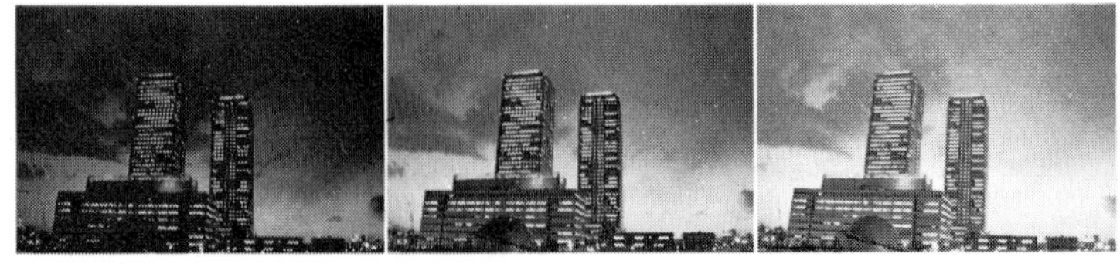

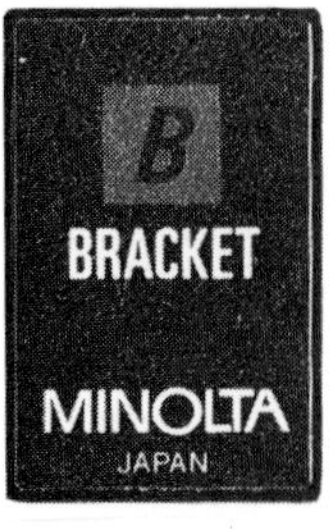

Creative Expansion Card for Exposure bracketing: The use of this card allows up to seven frames to be taken, the exposures can vary by either 1/3, 1/2 or whole exposure stop.

slightly underexposed; the colours appear deeper and more vivid. Professionals do not rely solely on their measurements and experience but have to take a sequence of frames to test the film material for a particular subject, varying the exposures systematically for each one. In this way they can be sure of obtaining the perfect exposure. The Minolta Dynax 8000i can take such exposure sequences automatically. Using the Exposure Bracketing card it is possible to take sequences of three, five or seven pictures, with exposure variations of a third, a half or a whole stop - one frame always being exposed with values that are considered correct by the camera. The camera is automatically set to continuous shooting mode as it is not possible to take such sequences in single frame mode. The automatic focus setting is stored from the first shot for the whole series.

To use, insert the card in the card door. The card name **brAc** will be displayed in the LCD panel together with its basic setting which is a shooting sequence of three frames with exposure differences of 0.5EV. To modify these settings, press the **CARD-ADJ** button. The display in the data panel will flash to indicate that the card is activated and that the exposure setting can now be changed via the setting control. It is possible to choose exposure compensations of 1/3, 1/2 or a full stop. As soon as the required values have been selected, press the **CARD** on/off key. **CARD** and a frame number will flash in the LCD panel. The possible sequence is either three, five or seven exposures and this is also changed by the setting control. To store the selected data press the **CARD-ADJ** button again. The variation in exposure and the number of exposures remain in memory until they are changed again. If data entry is interrupted for longer than 20 sec then the LCD

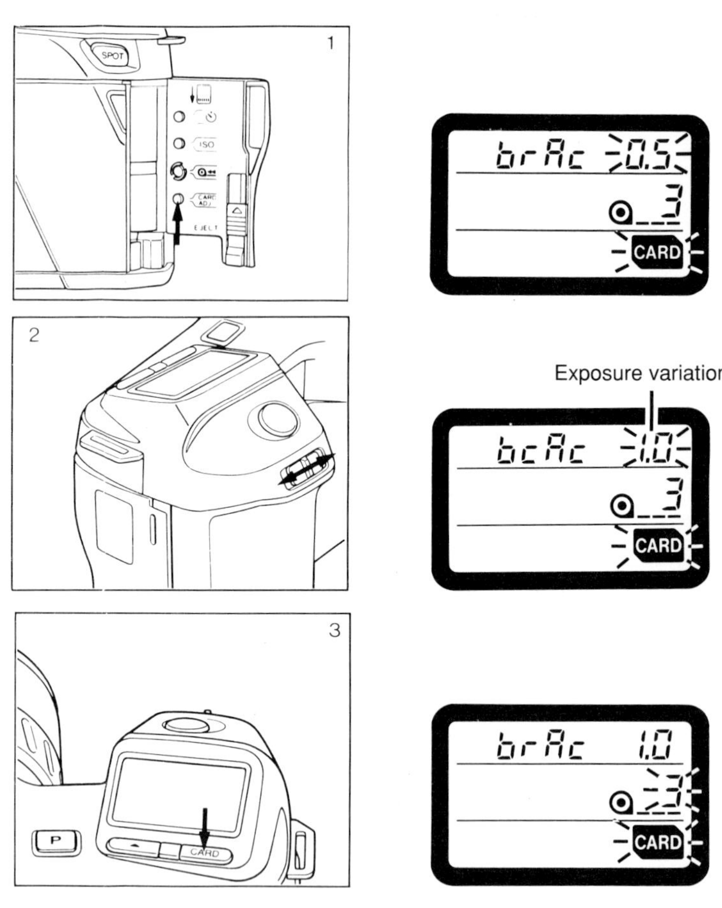

Changing the settings:

1. Open card door and press card-adjust button. The displays for card in use and exposure value flash and neither autofocus nor shutter release will function. If the exposure value is not to be changed go to step 3. key for card setting. The displays for card activated and EV-stops begin to blink. While this display blinks, neither the Af system, nor the shutter release will function. If no change in the exposure variation is required, go to step 3.
2. To change the exposure value, use the setting control to select 0.3, 0.5 or 1.0 EV. If the number of exposures is not to be changed go to step 5.
3. After the required exposure is set, press CARD on/off key. The displays for card in use and number of exposures will now flash in the data panel.

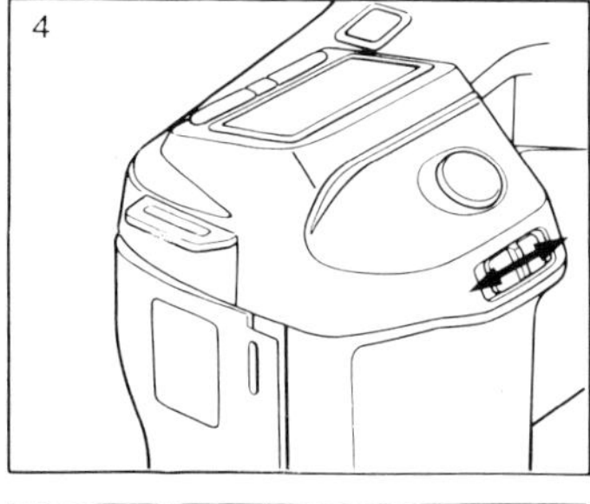

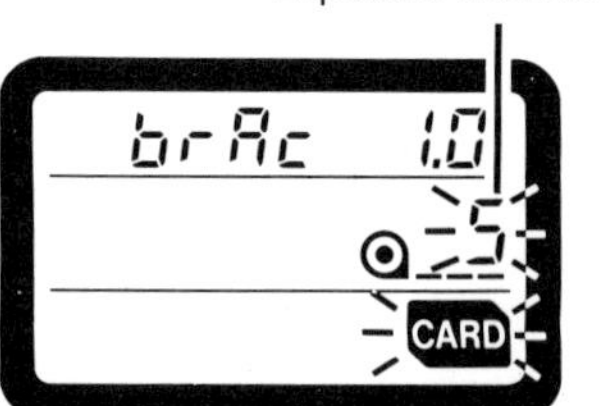

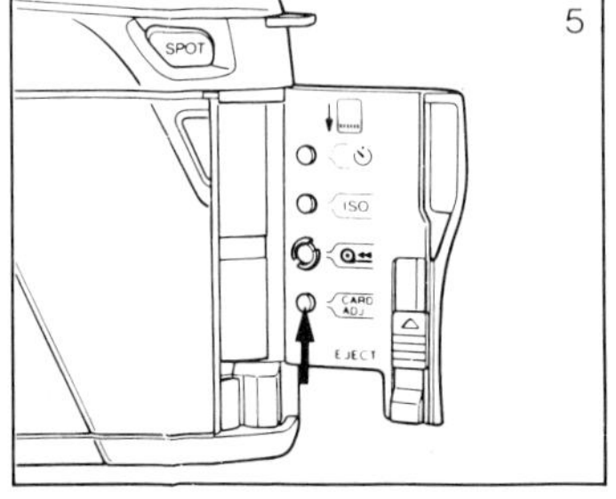

4. Select the number of exposures by setting control (3, 5 or 7 frames).
5. After the required number of frames is set, press the card-adj button again. This will store the selected values in memory until further amendment. If no changes are made within 20 seconds while the card is activated, the display reverts to normal and the previously-stored data remains in memory.
6. Close card door.

panel returns to normal display. The last entered data will then be activated again.

With the exception of the TTL flash mode, for which there is a another card, it is possible to take automatic exposure sequences in any of the exposure modes. In program mode both aperture and shutter speed are automatically controlled. In aperture priority mode, only the shutter speed is varied and in shutter speed priority, it is the aperture that is varied, to effect exposure compensations. If the camera is set to manual exposure, then the photographer may choose which of the two, the aperture or the shutter speed, should be varied. To select the variable, press the aperture-setting button to change the aperture, whilst taking the sequence, otherwise it is the shutter speed that will be varied. If the required shutter speeds or aperture values lie outside the available metering range of the camera, the Dynax 8000i will automatically select the available shutter speed/aperture combination.

Program Shift Card

Unlike the modifications effected by the card for automatic exposure bracketing where the exposure level is varied throughout the sequence, the Program Shift card allows the photographer to take a sequence of three correctly-exposed frames with different shutter speed/aperture combinations. The first shot is taken at the normal program setting. The Dynax 8000i measures the luminosity, subject position and focal length of the lens. The second exposure is then taken with a faster shutter speed and a larger aperture, the third with a smaller aperture and a slower shutter speed.

The amount by which the aperture and shutter speed are varied, can be determined by the photographer. This may be effected in one, two or three stops.

Whenever the program shift card is activated, the Dynax 8000i works in full program mode. It is not possible to choose any of the other exposure modes with this card. When the card is activated the word **SHFt** is displayed in the top line of the LCD panel, together with the shift size. Press the **CARD** on/off key and change the values using the setting control. Pressing the **CARD-ADJ** button will store the selected values.

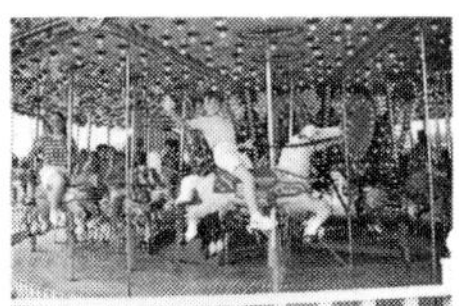
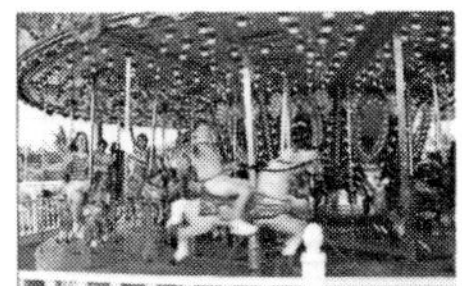
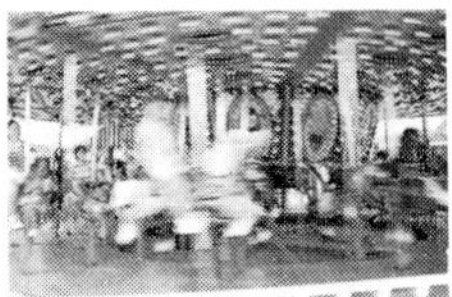

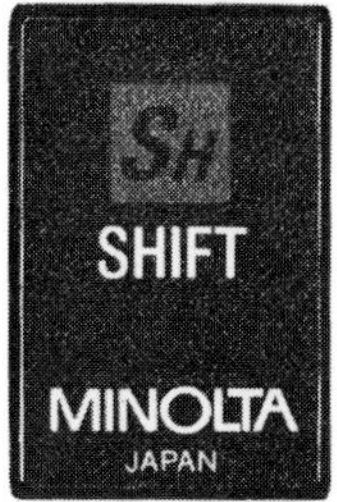

Creative Expansion Card for Automatic Program Shift: This card is used to shoot sequences with preset automatic program shift between each frame.

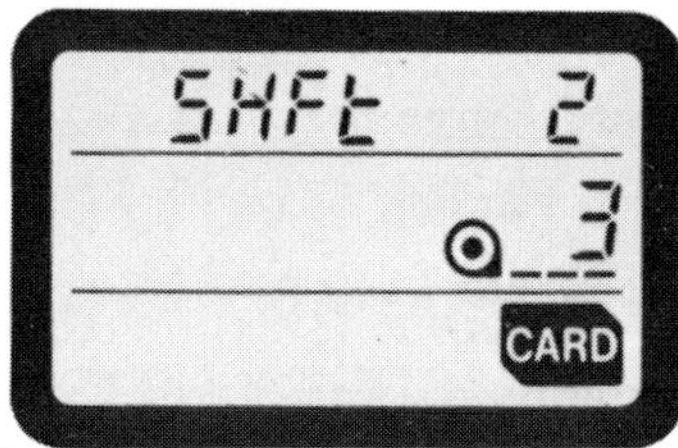

LCD panel with Automatic Program Shift Card in use.

If the selected values are to be changed again, this button has to be pressed again. This card is particularly useful for photo reportage assignments, when experimentation by manual setting is too slow and risky, because it removes the element of risk and speeds up shooting. For example, at a ski-jumping competition it is possible to show the competitors in sharp focus with a fast shutter speed as well as speed-blurred with a much slower shutter speed. As the three shots are taken at short intervals, you will not miss the opportunity and are assured of a good shot.

Highlight/Shadow Control Card

"All theory is grey" according to Goethe (Faust). This applies in more ways than one to exposure metering in photography. Our cameras are programmed on the assumption that the reflectivity of the metered subject corresponds to that of an average grey. Reality is somewhat different though. Thankfully life is not all grey but quite colourful and, apart from their reflectivity, all colours possess their own basic brightness. To assess correct exposure, it is not only necessary to assess the illumination of the subject but also its intrinsic colour. If I am trying to shoot a subject that lies outside the six segment metering area of the Dynax 8000i, against a black background, then the camera would consider this to be a poorly lit grey background because it reflects less light than an average grey one. The camera would compensate for the supposedly poor light and overexpose the picture. This is particularly noticeable with bright subjects in front of a dark background. In the case of normally structured subjects, the multi-pattern metering control combined with the autofocus control would recognize such differences in brightness and adjust its function accordingly. Alternatively, the photographer measures the subject by using the centre focus area and spot-metering button, stores the values and realigns the camera to select the required frame. Under special circumstances, i.e. if the subject is a monochrome scene, it is still possible to obtain under- or overexposures. The use of the Highlight/Shadow Control card ensures that an important highlight will be recorded as a highlight and an important shadow area or a dark tone will be that rather than a mid-tone. It allows for spot metering which also takes into account the surface characteristic of the metered subject. If the light parts are metered, and the card is programmed appropriately, then the Dynax 8000i will automatically overexpose by 2.3 stops, whilst if the shadow parts are measured, then the camera will underexpose by 2.7 stops. The Highlight/shadow control card is automatically activated as soon as it is inserted in the card door. In the first line of the data panel **HIGH** is displayed, being the abbreviation for highlight. This means that the Dynax 8000i performs highlight-orientated spot metering. To change to shadow-orientated metering, first press the **CARD-ADJ** button and then the **CARD** on/off key to actually make the selection. Now the display in the first line of the data panel is **SHAd,** the abbreviation for shadow. This function can be cancelled by pressing the **CARD** on/off key and the card will be deactivated even if left in the card door.

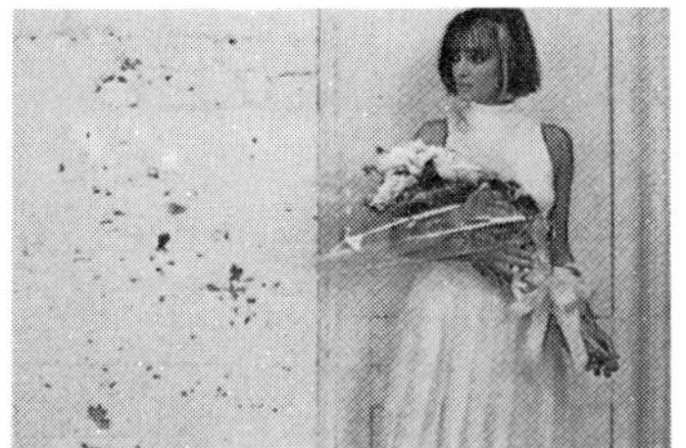
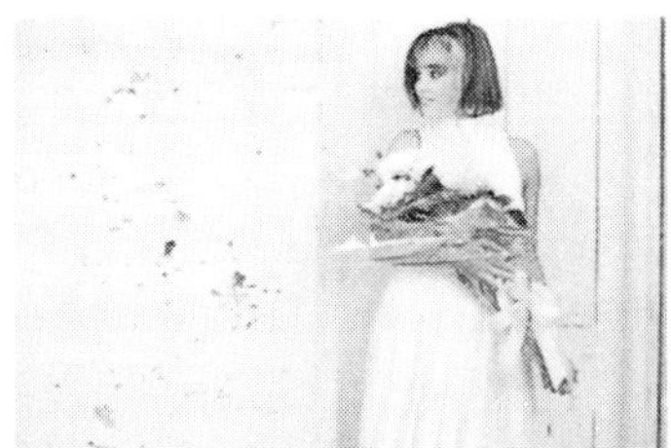
With highlight orientated spot metering

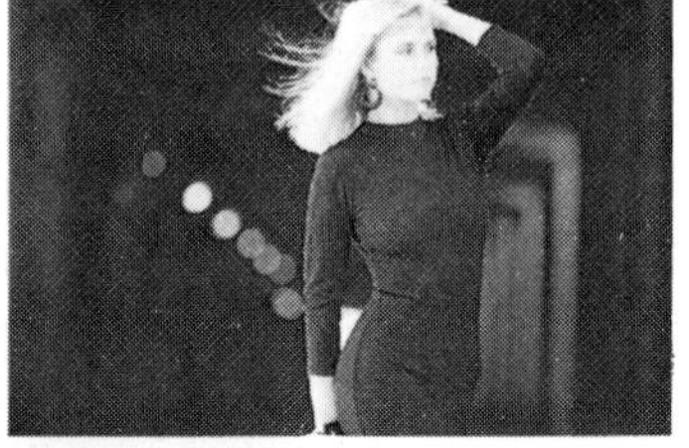
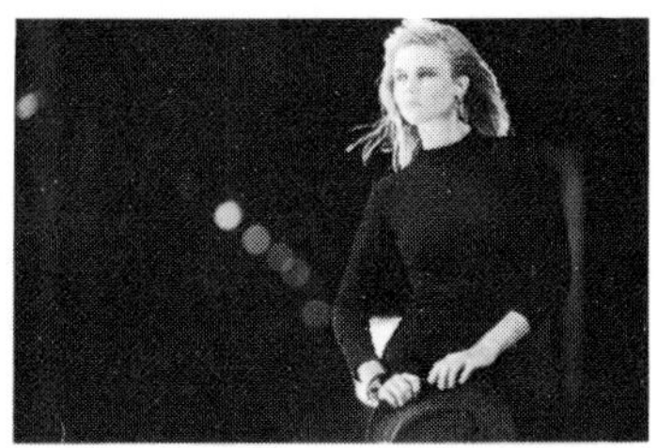
With shadow orientated spot metering

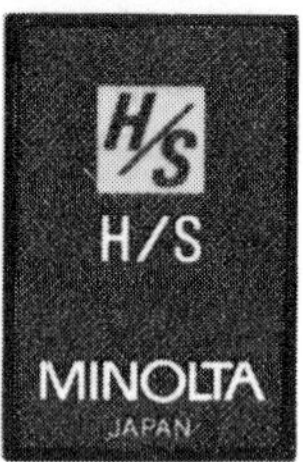

Creative Expansion Card for Highlight/Shadow Control: This card allows exposures with spot metering biased towards either the highlights or the shadows in difficult lighting conditions.

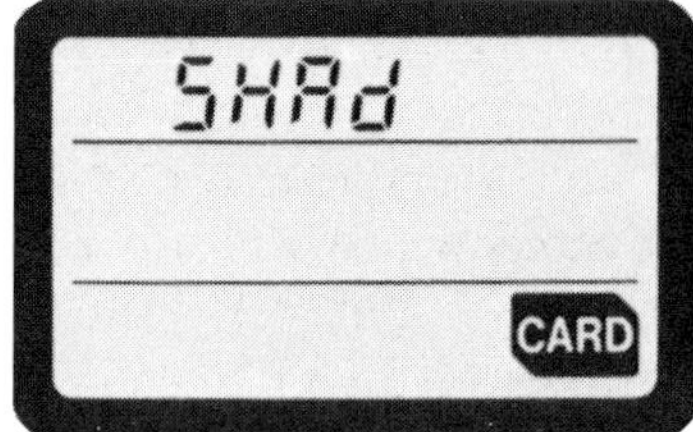

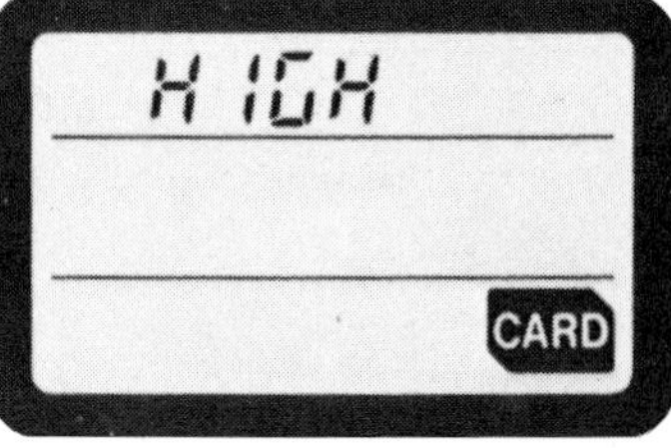

LCD panel showing Highlight/Shadow Control Card in use; shadow evaluation (left) or highlight evaluation (right).

Multiple Exposure Card

This card was specially developed for the Dynax 8000i and allows the automatic exposure of up to nine exposures on one frame. Before using this facility, even though it is possible to use three different exposure modes, it is a good idea to understand something about multiple exposure. The main problem is that the partial exposure is not necessarily determined by the number of total exposures, but by the number of superimposed images on the frame. If, for example, a person is taken eight times, to be shown "standing in a row" against a dark background, each exposure should receive the normal amount of light. However, if the images overlap, then it is necessary to calculate a compensation. The amount by which the normal exposure is compensated depends on the number of superimpositions. Staying with our example, if the images overlap only once then the exposure has to be calculated like a double exposure. However, if the eight individual images are superimposed to produce two groups of four, then the multiple exposure has to be corrected as for a four-times exposure. The number of the superimposed exposures is the factor which, multiplied with the set ISO value, results in the new "assumed" film speed which is set to take an automatically controlled shot. If the background is bright, then this has to be assessed as an extra factor and allowed for accordingly in the calculation of the film speed. This is the simplest method for multiple exposures, to which a slight minus compensation should still be applied. As you can see, taking multiple exposures is not that easy and this is the reason why the Multiple Exposure card offers two technically-simplified variations.

The Multiple Exposure card always assumes that it

New Creative Expansion Card for Multiple Exposures: Up to nine exposures can be taken on one frame, in three different modes: normal, "fade-in" and "fade-out".

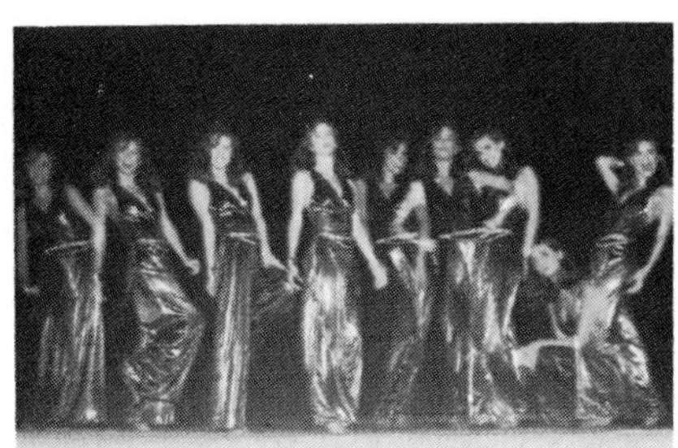

is dealing with a normal multiple exposure situation (dark background with subject(s) depicted next to each other), without any superimpositions, as far as the exposure is concerned. For this reason the partial exposures all receive the normal amount of light - i.e. they are exposed with the values that are displayed in the viewfinder. If the "fade-out" and "fade-in" functions are used, then the partial exposures are either increasingly over- or underexposed. The first partial exposure in "fade-out" and the last partial exposure in "fade-in" are again normally exposed. This techniques allows a subject to be shown with increasing or decreasing intensity.

Flash Bracketing Card

This card can be used to program the camera for flash sequences of three, five or seven individual exposures, with differences in exposure between each frame of either half or a full stop. The first frame is always taken at the "normal" reading, frame two is always overexposed by the predetermined amount, with frame three underexposed by the same amount. Therefore, the main subject in frames two, four and six is always increasingly overexposed by half or a full stop, and in frames three, five and seven, the main subject is always increasingly underexposed by the same amounts. This over- and underexposure by increased or decreased flash output refers always to the main subject, which is the speciality of this particular programming function. This is possible because the exposure metering system (camera set to P or S mode) takes a reading of the background before every exposure; this results in the background always being equally bright with only the main subject in the foreground illuminated differently. The control of the exposure is performed by the TTL flash metering system, the set aperture and flash synchronization speeds remain activated. This method also works in combination with slow shutter sync (camera set to P or A mode) if the spot-metering button is used to meter a subject detail in the background.

This particular effect is achieved by controlling the flash duration which influences the flash range. In the case of a plus compensation, when more light is required, the flash range would be reduced, and for a minus compensation the flash range is extended. For a compensation of half a stop the conversion factor for the new flash range is 0.7 and for a full stop it is 1.4. The

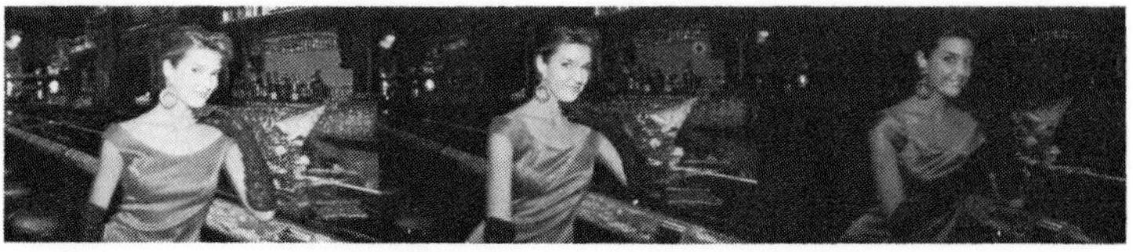

New Creative Expansion Card for Flash Bracketing: This card allows a sequence of flashed exposures, each frame receiving a different amount of flash illumination. A sequence of 3, 5 or 7 frames can be taken with exposure variations of 1/2 or full stops. This card automatically performs complicated functions that used to require the expert knowledge of an experienced photographer.

LCD panels of Program Flash 5200i and 4000AF show the selected flash range for every frame, with the normal flash range being displayed after each exposure. All these variables have no influence on the closest subject distance.

In this mode, the camera will only take one frame at a time, even if it is set to continuous shooting mode. If you take your finger off the release, then the difference in exposures and the number of the next frame is displayed for about 5 seconds. Short, fast flashing between frames indicates that the previous frame has been correctly illuminated. If the release is pressed before the flash is properly charged - indicated by the slow flashing of the flash-ready symbol in the viewfinder - then the flash is not triggered but the film is wound on for the next frame in the sequence. However, this does not apply if Program Flash 1800AF, 2800AF or 4000AF is attached; these will always be triggered, regardless of whether they are properly recharged or not. Program flashguns cannot be set to the reduced output "LO". If the output of the flash used is too high or too low, it could be possible that the complete flashed sequence is not taken; it is therefore more sensible to set the exposure difference to half a stop for longer sequences. After the sequence has been taken, the legend "end" appears for 5 seconds in the LCD panel.

Multi Spot Memory Card

Spot metering always produces the most precise result. However, this method quite often produces unintended results, as it is only too easy to pick the wrong subject detail for metering. To use spot metering correctly requires a good knowledge of exposure metering principles in all illumination situations and for all

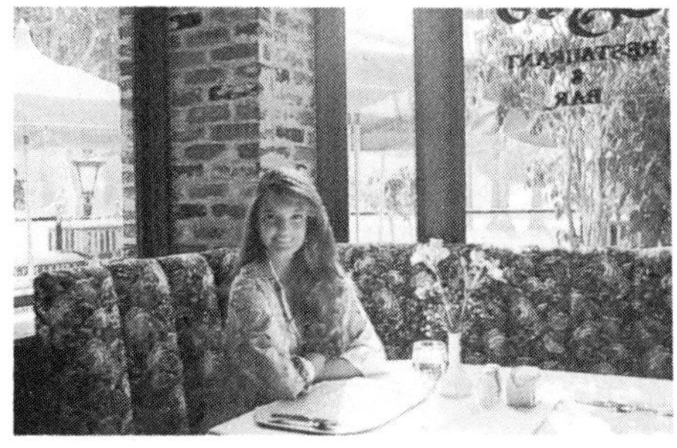

With multi-spot metering

Without multi-spot metering

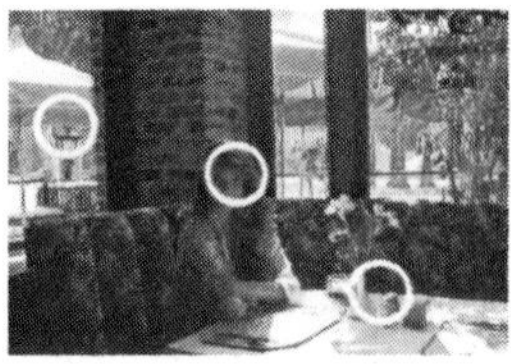

New Creative Expansion Card for Multi-Spot Memory: This card fulfils the most demanding requirements in the most difficult exposure situations. The average value is calculated from the different metering results and the appropriate exposure values set.

types of subjects. This Creative Expansion card can help you overcome some of the pitfalls; moreover it is of interest to the photographer who wishes to use multiple readings to produce certain effects. The use of this card allows up to eight spot metering results to be stored which are used by the camera to calculate an average value. This is then used for all subsequent exposures, until the card is deactivated. This average metering result remains in memory even after the camera has been switched off and returned to the ON position.

This card is inserted in the card door, just like all the others, and **SPOT** appears for 5 seconds in the LCD panel.

Now the release is pressed lightly and the lens is focused on the main subject. Then the first subject detail is metered by placing the central spot-metering circle over the appropriate area (the lens is not refocused) and the spot-metering button is pressed with the thumb to store the value. This may be repeated up to eight times, the camera calculating every time the new average value, the appropriate aperture/

shutter speed combination appearing in the data panel. Also displayed next to the word **SPOT** is the number of meterings that have already been taken. Should you attempt to take more than eight measurements they will not be taken into account. If a wrong subject detail is metered by mistake the whole process has to be cancelled by pressing the **CARD** on/off key.

The Multi Spot Memory card can be used in conjunction with exposure modes P, A, S or M.

In P mode the camera will automatically set both the aperture and shutter speed according to the average calculated value and the multi-program exposure curve, that takes the focal length of the attached lens into account. It is then possible to use program shift to select a different aperture/shutter speed combination without changing the ascertained exposure level.

In A mode, when the aperture has been preselected, the camera will automatically select a suitable shutter speed to agree with the calculated exposure result. In case a shutter speed outside the camera's available range is necessary, the aperture will automatically be adjusted to allow a suitable shutter speed to be set. This eventuality is indicated by the flashing display of the shutter speed. This process can also be adjusted manually using the setting control. Program shift is also possible in this shooting mode.

The behaviour of the camera is similar in S mode, when the shutter speed had been preselected. Now this will be automatically adjusted, if the resulting aperture is out of range for the calculated exposure value. Again, the aperture value will flash to indicate automatic adjustment.

If the camera is set to manual operation (M mode), then the difference between the manual and the calculated settings is displayed. Now the photographer can adjust either aperture or shutter speed, or both, to bring the settings into alignment with the calculated average value.

With this card activated it is possible to set the camera to either the single frame or continuous frame shooting modes - regardless of which exposure mode is selected. However, flash is not possible. The card can only be activated if an attached flash unit is switched off.

Note: the average value, once ascertained, will be held in memory and reapplied as long as the card is activated.

Data Memory Card

In experimental work, if certain sequences have to be repeated exactly, records of shooting data are invaluable to professionals and amateurs alike. The Minolta Dynax 8000i will keep these records for you automatically with the aid of the data memory card. It is capable of remembering, simultaneously, six different shooting data for up to 40 exposures, and these may be recalled at any time. The following shooting data may be stored - shooting mode, shutter speed, aperture, focal length and maximum aperture of attached lens, and any exposure compensations if appropriate. When the film has been completely exposed, the data may be recalled and noted down for later reference. Naturally, it is possible to recall the stored data at any time while the film is still in the camera.

As soon as the card is activated, **dAtA** appears in the first line of the LCD panel and **CARD** appears in the third line. The stored data are displayed on recall in

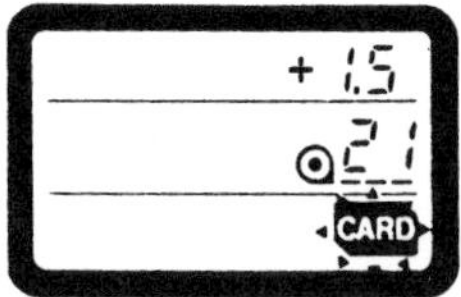

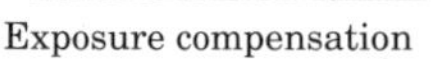

Exposure compensation

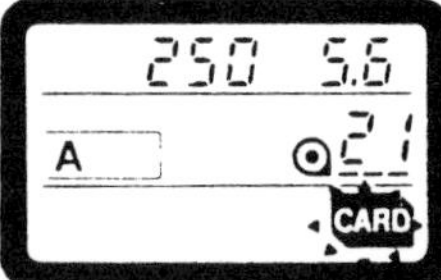

Exposure mode, shutter speed and aperture

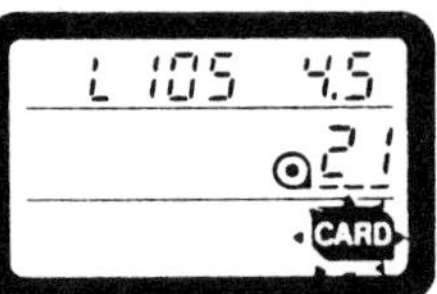

Lens focal length and speed

The LCD panel showing the various data can be recalled with the Data Memory Card.

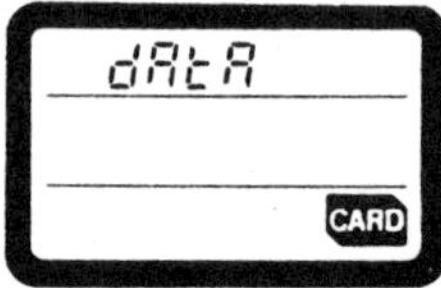

Creative Expansion Card for Data Memory: important shooting data, such as shutter speed, aperture, any exposure compensation, lens specification or frame number can be stored and recalled with this card.

three different combinations. By pressing the **CARD** on/off key they will be displayed one after the other in the data panel, the card display flashing at the same time. The sequence is as follows: shutter speed and aperture values are displayed in the top line of the panel, the exposure mode is shown in the second line. Pressing the **CARD** on/off key again will display the focal length of the lens used and its maximum aperture. If the shot is taken with a zoom lens, the actual focal length will be displayed. The number of the frame you wish to check is selected by the setting control.

To catch the right moment with your camera requires a good eye, quick reaction and a lot of patience. The intelligent program mode of the Dynax 8000i, in connection with the multi-pattern metering system, guarantees perfect snapshots.

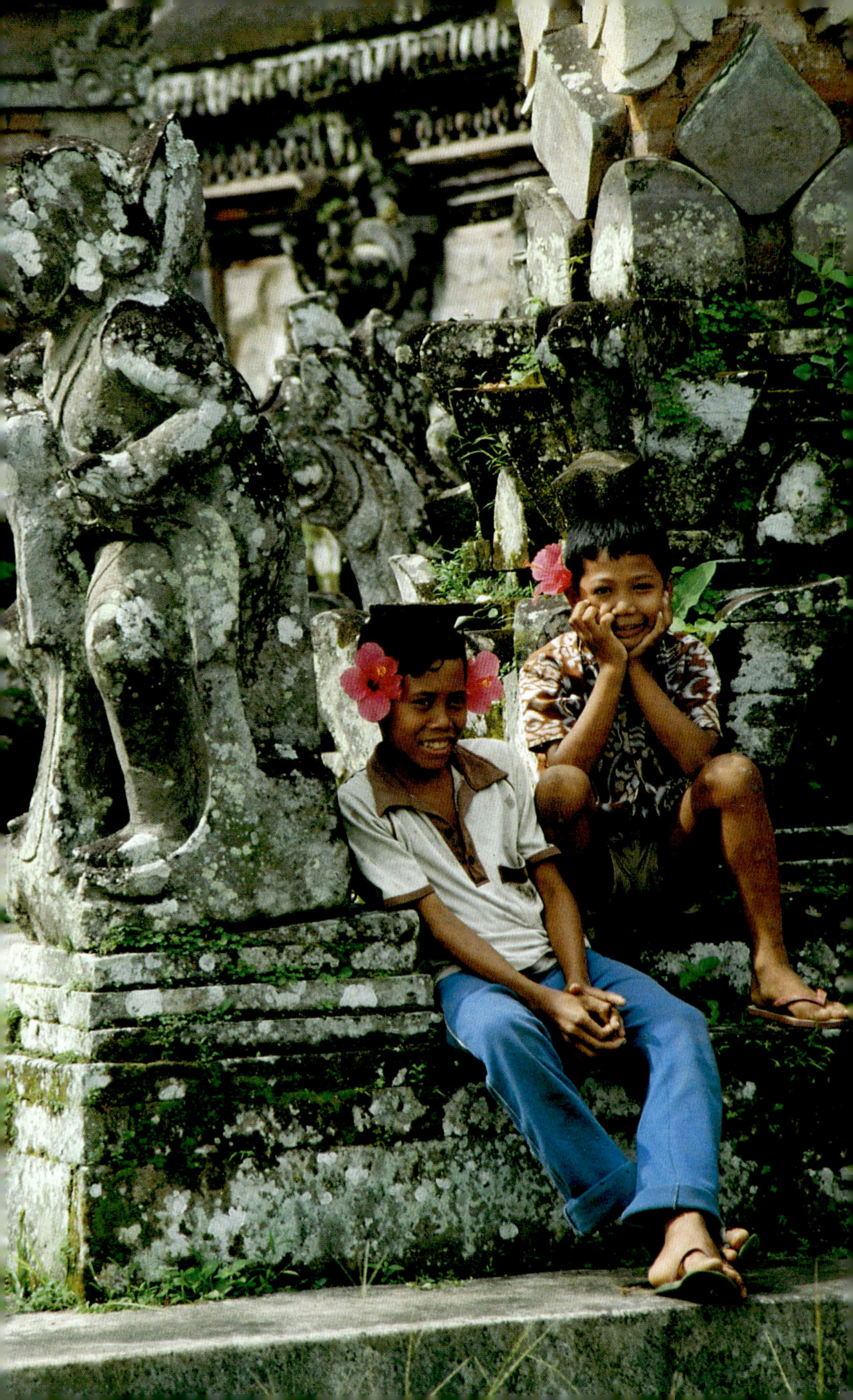

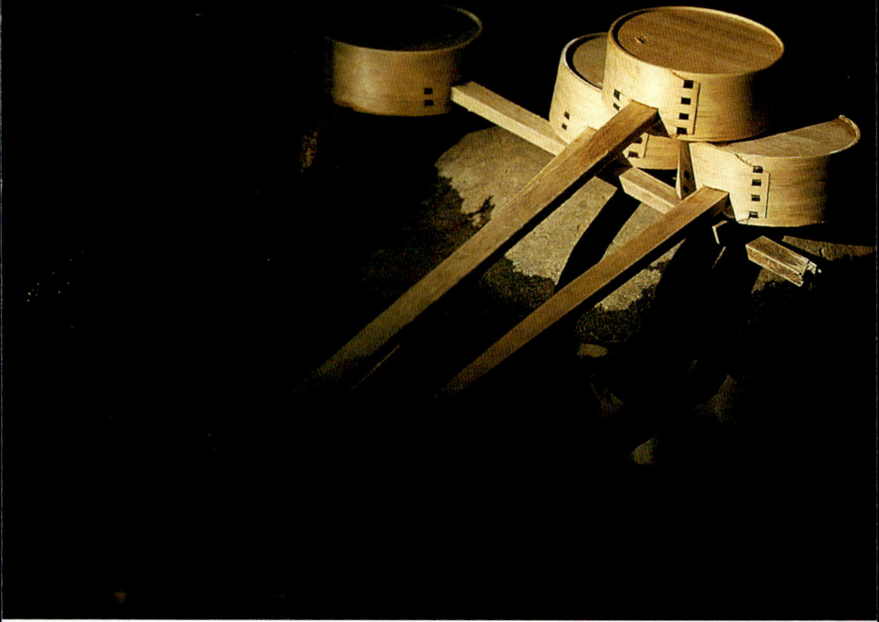

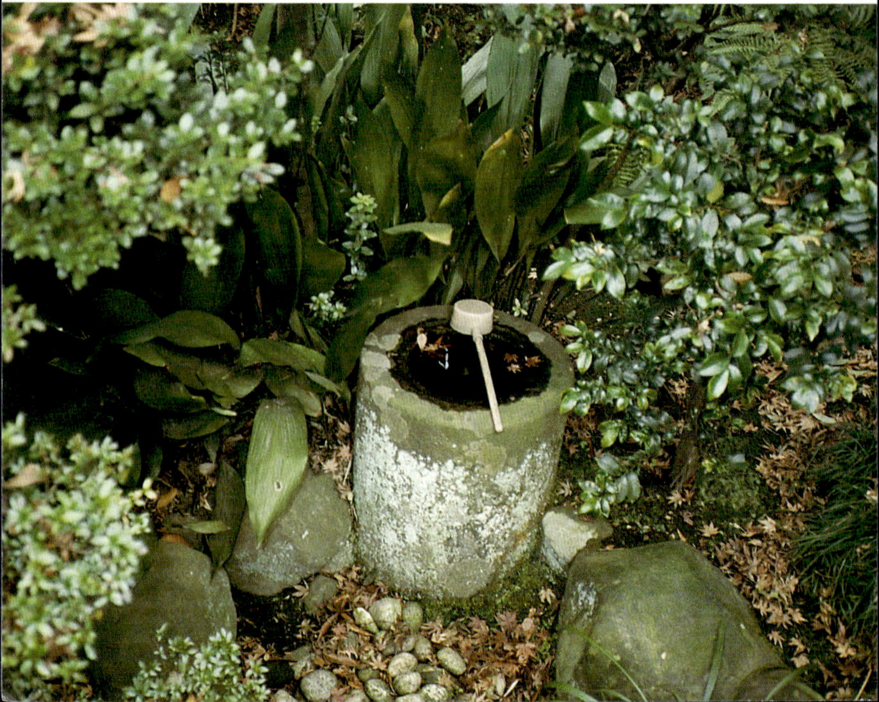

Fantasy Effect Card

Professional photographers often use a special trick to achieve a moody soft-focus look which is rather difficult but very effective if handled carefully. They don't use a soft-focus filter instead achieving a stunning effect by double exposure. The shot is taken as usual in sharp focus but for the second exposure the lens is set slightly out of focus to produce a soft halo. How much the lens must be set out of focus has to be ascertained by experiment. With this card activated, the Dynax 8000i automatically adjusts the focus slightly during the exposure to achieve the desired effect without having to make a double exposure. The card saves you the cumbersome calculations involved in working out the exposure and adjusting the focus of the lens. The actual effect will depend on the depth of field.

Another effect can be achieved by using an "i" series flash. When the card is initially switched on it will deactivate the flash. The flash must therefore be switched back on manually. Thereafter it will fire each time the shutter is released. The illumination freezes the sharp outline of the object against a speed-blurred background.

Program shift is not possible with the fantasy card nor will the camera emit an audible warning signal for too long exposure times. The fantasy effect can also not be used with the macro setting on zoom lenses which

---

⇦ *Typical subjects for the spot metering method, because in these cases it was important to lay the emphasis on a particular subject detail.*

This Feature Card produces desired fantastic effects without the need for special filters.

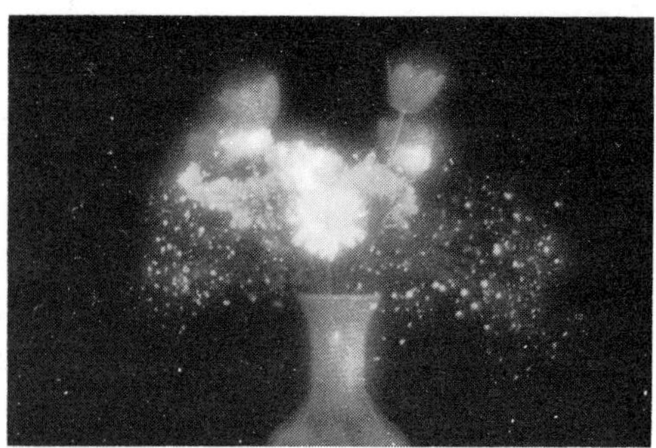

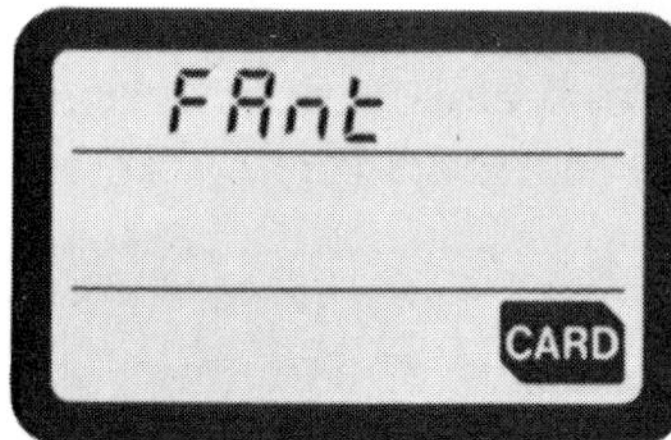

LDC panel showing Fantasy Effect Card in use.

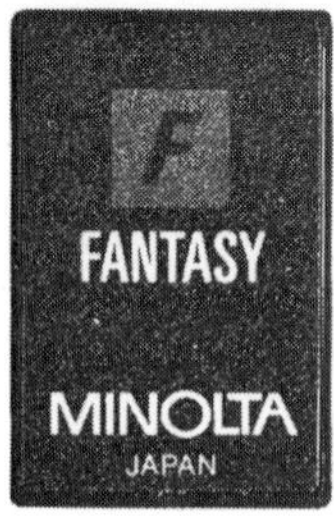

Creative Expansion Card for Fantasy Effect: This card creates special effects automatically for unusual results.

have a separate macro switch, and the focus-stop button on the lens should also not be used.

When the card is activated, the first line of the data panel displays **FAnt** and the bottom line **CARD.** If the subject is either too dark or too bright the legend **LO** or **HI** flashes and the release will be locked. In the former case you may have to change the film for a faster one or, for the latter case, use a neutral density filter to solve the problem.

Special Application Cards

These cards influence the basic exposure programs, the autofocus function and the film transport to tailor the camera's program mode for specialized requirements. Other exposure modes are not possible when one of these cards is activated. This has the advantage that no other settings have to be made. All necessary variations are automatically calculated and passed to the main computer in the Dynax 8000i. Cards in this category are offered for sports and action photography, portrait photography, close-up photography and for photography where depth of field is of particular importance.

Sports Action Card

Sport and action photography requires fast shutter speeds to avoid movement blur. Fast reactions by the photographer is another essential requirement. He and his camera have to be ready at the decisive moment because generally there is no time to make cumbersome adjustments. It does not matter whether you wish to catch the high jumper at the peak of his leap across the bar, a bird in flight, or the surfer on the crest of the wave, your concentration on the right moment and frame should not be diverted by exposure calculations. In such situations the Sports Action card will be a most welcome tool.

This card programs the Dynax 8000i to select the fastest possible shutter speeds with reference to the focal length and distance setting. It is not possible to use other exposure modes when this card is activated. The **CARD** on/off key is used to choose between program mode with fast shutter speeds and normal operation. When the card is activated, the normal program shift is inactive but the continuous autofocus mode is activated to follow the moving subject at all times. Manual focusing is possible in this mode, but whether it makes sense to use it is a different matter. A further special function of this card is that it automatically switches off the flashgun. If flash is required, it has to be activated manually by the switch on the flashgun. It will only operate for poorly lit subjects, it will not trigger to fill-in backlit subjects. To suppress the triggering of automatic flash seems a very sensible arrangement. Let's consider the situation when fill-in flash is activated for against-the-light shots. The shutter speed would be automatically set to the flash synchronization speed of 1/125 sec. This would be much too slow for fast action shots and cause movement blur. Then you have to consider that by necessity most sport and action photographs have to be taken from a distance which would exceed the illumination range of the flashgun.

For sports and action photography with this card the use of faster films is recommended to allow the program mode full scope to set the required fast shutter speeds for freezing rapid movements.

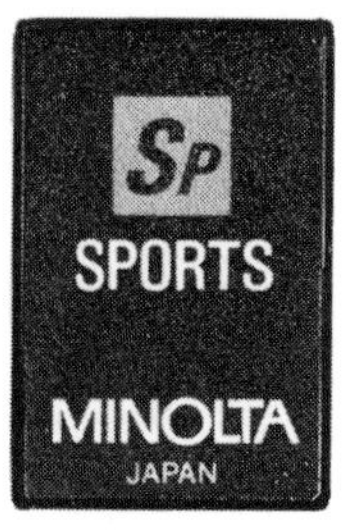

Creative Expansion Card for Sports Action: The use of this card favours fast shutter speeds to freeze fast movements.

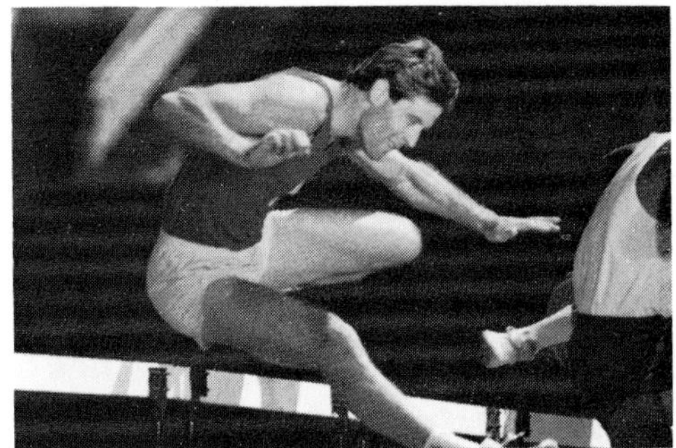

Fast movements require fast shutter speeds to avoid movement blur. This Special Application card automatically selects them.

When the card is inserted, **SPrt** appears in the top line of the data panel and **CARD** in the bottom line to show that the card is active. This function may be cancelled at any time by pressing the **CARD** on/off key, which returns the Dynax 8000i to normal shooting modes. Removal of the card will also cancel the special functions.

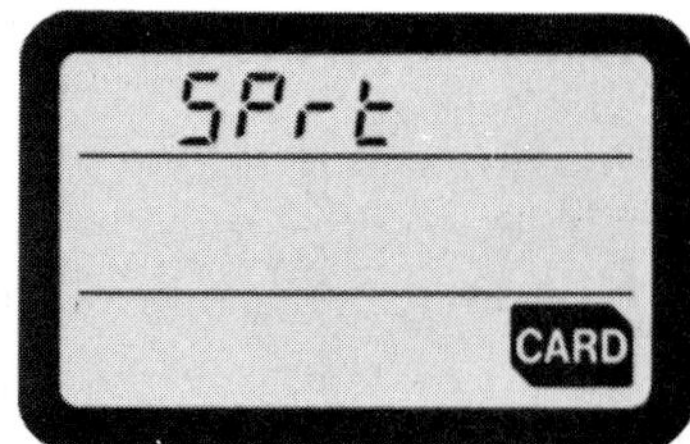

The LCD panel showing the Sports Action Card in use.

Automatic Depth Control Card

When the lens is focused on a subject, objects at a certain distance in front of and behind the subject will also appear sharp in the photograph. This range within which the three-dimensional subject space is depicted in reasonably sharp focus is called depth of field. The depth of field depends on the shooting distance, the focal length of the lens and the aperture. A short focal length, long shooting distance and small aperture produces a wide depth of field, whereas a long focal length, short shooting distance and large aperture produce a narrow depth of field. It was necessary on earlier SLRs to check the depth of field by the aperture stop-down (or depth of field preview) button. The Minolta Dynax 8000i has no such button. Instead, the

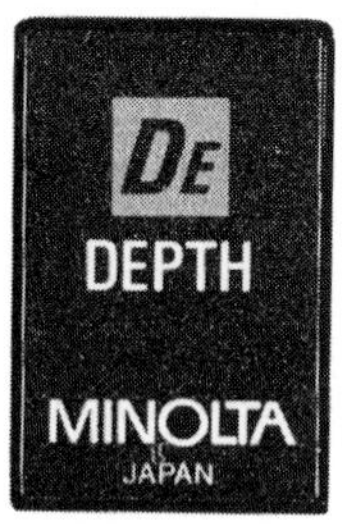

Creative Expansion Card for Automatic Depth Control: This card controls the aperture in relationship to the focus setting to ensure maximum depth of field.

This special feature card ensures a large depth of field, to bring the main subject as well as the background into sharp focus.

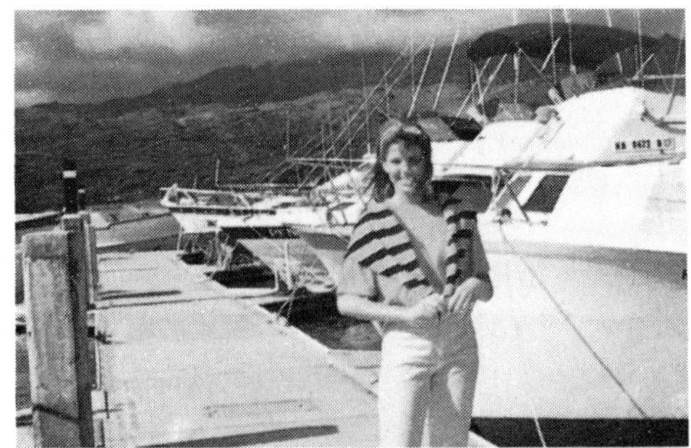

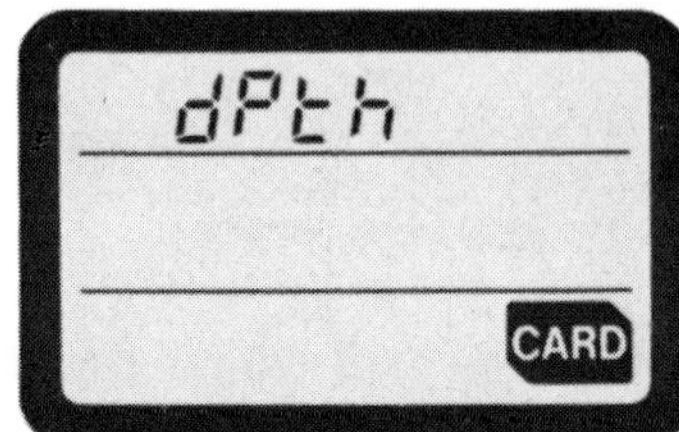

The LCD panel with the Automatic Depth Control Card in use.

automatic depth control card is used to program the aperture and focusing plane to produce maximum depth of field.

Insert the card in the card door. In the first line of the data panel **dPth** will appear, with **CARD** in the bottom line. The card function can be cancelled by pressing the **CARD** on/off key. When this card is activated the Dynax 8000i will automatically set itself to program mode and it is not possible to use other shooting modes. Program shift is also blocked, as a change in the exposure values would influence the automatically-optimised depth of field. The predictive autofocus function is also not possible. The AF function initially sets the focus at infinity because the focusing paths are much shorter for the further focusing ranges, i.e. from 3 metres, than for the close-up range. How large the depth of field is also depends on the lighting conditions.

If a large aperture is necessary to cope with poor light, it could result in an unsharp background. The Automatic Depth Control card does not precisely calculate the space within which the subject is supposed to be sharp, like most other system designs, instead it maximises the space behind the subject so that it will be shown in sharp focus. This card is particularly suitable for landscapes and architectural shots. For macro photography, which is another subject where depth of field is critical, Minolta have designed a separate card.

Closeup Card

The depth of field shrinks dramatically with an increasing reproduction scale, i.e. the ratio between the actual subject size and its reproduction on film. This fact is taken into account by the Closeup card for the Minolta Dynax 8000i. Depending on the reproduction ratio it will control the aperture to obtain an appropriate depth of field. As soon as the card is inserted, the camera is switched to automatic program mode and the autofocus is set to normal AF function, without predictive focusing. **CLOS UP** appears in the top line of the data panel, with **CARD** in the bottom line. It is not possible to use the Dynax in any other shooting mode with this card activated. Unlike programming for depth of field, where it is extended into the background, this card is programmed to select an aperture appropriate to the magnification ratio of the subject. The resulting shutter speeds are monitored and chosen to ensure hand-held shots free from camera shake.

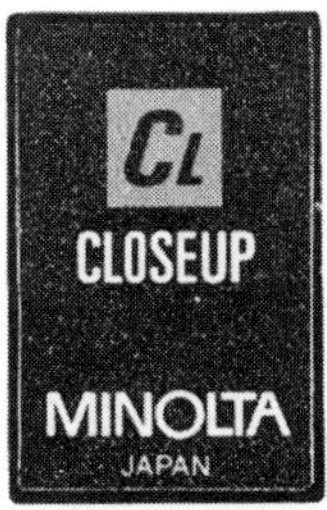

Creative Expansion Card for Closeups: this card controls the aperture for optimum depth of field.

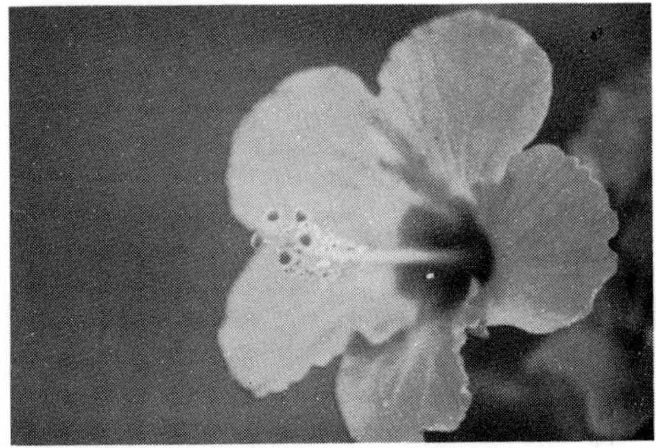

In close-up photography it is necessary to stop down the aperture as much as possible to obtain a suitable depth of field. This is rather limited for increasingly larger reproduction ratios. This Special Application card will do it automatically for you.

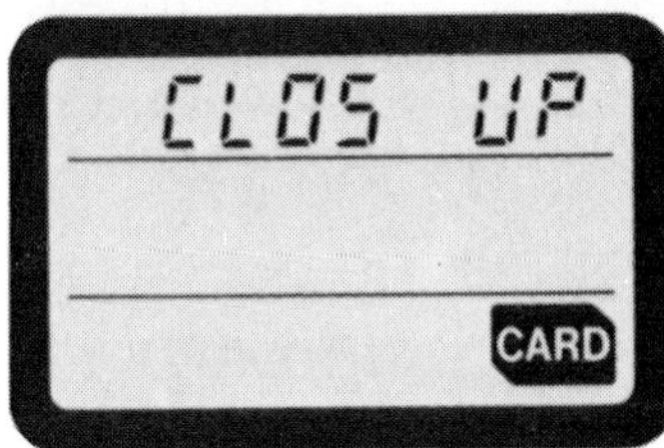

LCD panel showing Closeup Card in use.

Portrait Card

As with the cards for automatic depth of field control and close-up photography, this card for portrait photography also uses depth of field as its creative medium. But contrary to the above two areas of photography, in portraiture it is desirable to work with a rather shallow depth of field, contrasting the main subject with a blurred and indistinct background. The choice of shutter speeds automatically takes into account the focal length of the attached lens to obtain hand-held shots free from camera shake.

After inserting the card, **Port** appears in the first line of the data panel with **CARD** in the bottom line. Pressing the **CARD** on/off key will cancel the card and reset the camera's functions to normal shooting modes.

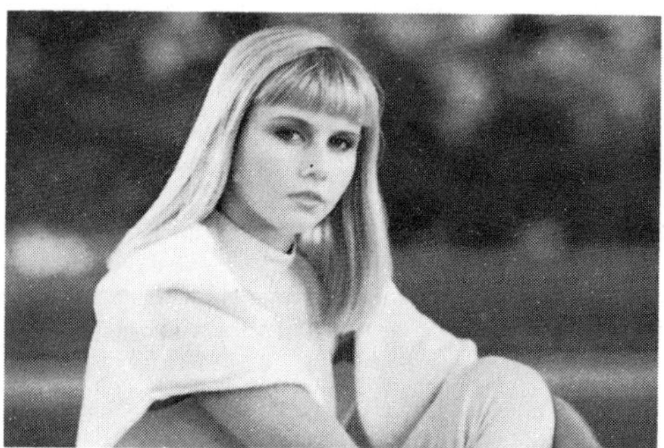

When a large aperture is selected, the background is out of depth of field and becomes a blurred backdrop; this is particularly useful for portrait photography as it sets the main subject effectively against the undefined background. This Special Application Card automatically ensures that a suitable aperture is chosen.

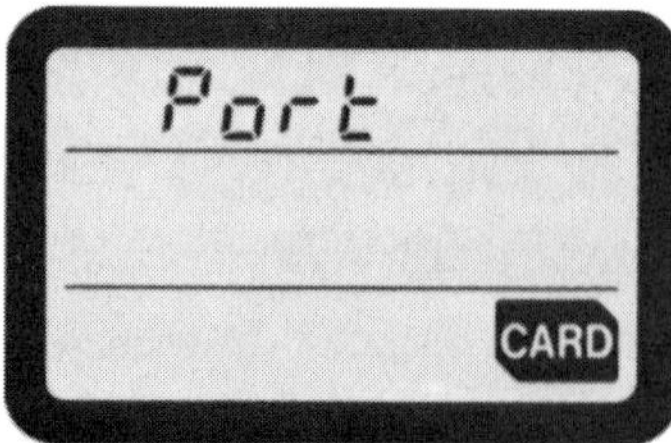

LCD panel with Portrait Card in use.

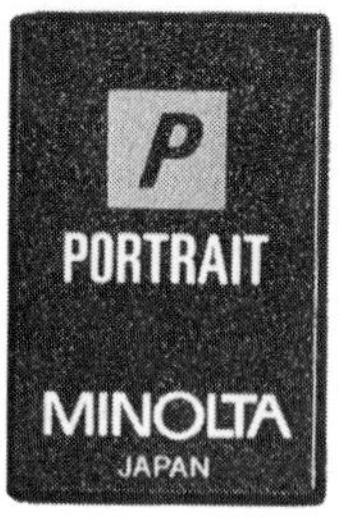

Creative Expansion Card for Portraits: this card is programmed to control typical exposure values (aperture/shutter speed) for portrait photography.

System Accessories for the Dynax 8000i

Program Back PB-7

The automatic identification of frames in a photographic sequence is not only essential for scientific and experimental purposes, it is also useful for keeping a record of holidays and events. With the Minolta Program Back PB-7 it is possible to expose automatically one of four different blocks of data. The choice includes the date in three different notations; the selected sequence of month and day are identified on the LCD panel of the program back under **D** for day and **M** for month. The preferred notations may be determined by the photographer and it is either year/month/day, month/day/year or day/month/year.

The time of day in hours and minutes, together with the day can be imprinted instead of the date. The program back possesses a 24-hour clock for this purpose.

To adjust any of these imprints, press the SET button and the data display will flash to indicate that it can be adjusted. Move the setting control to increase or decrease the displayed values. To store the new value and select the next one for adjustment press the **SET** button again. The exposure of the selected data can always be cancelled by pressing the **PRINT ON/OFF** button. If this function is activated, the word **PRINT** appears in the LCD panel of the program back. If date imprint is selected then **DATE** appears and **TIME** will appear next to **PRINT** for time imprint.

Imprints of automatically-increasing six-digit numbers can be programmed instead of the date or time. This function is also selected by the **SET** button and is indicated on the LCD panel by **COUNT.** The number increases by one with each frame. There is also a six-digit code number which does not change between frames. With the **SET** button select **FIXNo** and a code. Subsequent changes of the code number have to be entered manually. The data is always imprinted in the bottom right-hand corner of the frame.

Intervalometer Function: Data imprinting is only one of the functions the Program Back PB-7 is capable of. The intervalometer function permits the photographer to set up the camera, program the starting time with intervals between exposures and leave. The

Dynax 8000i, triggered into action by the Program Back PB-7, will do the rest. It automatically selects the exposure values, sets the focus and if flash is to be used, recharges and triggers the flash unit.

The Dynax will automatically activate the release precisely when it was programmed to; on any day within one month. To activate this function press the **INT** button and **INTERVAL START** appears in the LCD panel, with **D** for day and a digital clock. The values for the interval can be entered when **INTERVAL TIME** appears in the LCD panel. The intervals may be chosen to the exact second. The largest interval between shots is 99 hours, 59 minutes and 59 seconds.

The last entry is the number of frames that have to be exposed. The choice can be made anywhere between 1 and 99. If more than 35 exposures are to be made the time between the shots has to be sufficient to allow a change of film. At present there are no film cassettes with more than 36 exposures available for 35mm cameras.

Long Exposure Function: The basic exposure control of the Dynax 8000i allows long, automatically-controlled, exposures of up to 30 sec. The use of the Program Back allows very long exposures at any time between 1 second and 9 hours 59 minutes and 59 seconds. Theoretically one could trace the tracks of stars from a certain date through 99 nights, provided, of course, that each one of these nights is dark and clear and that the film is changed, but the battery is unlikely to last. To select these very long exposures, the LCD panels shows **INTERVAL L.TIME,** and beneath that is the display for hours, minutes and seconds.

To abort an interval sequence, press the special **INT START/STOP** button on the Program Back, pressing this button again will restart it. If data imprinting is also required, this is activated by the **PRINT ON/OFF** button.

Data Back DB-7

This Data Back is only capable of data imprinting. As with the Program Back PB-7, the date may be chosen from three different notations, namely year/month/day, month/day/year or day/month/year. The positions are identified by **MONTH** and **DAY** beneath the appropriate numbers in the LCD panel. The **PRINT** display will indicate whether data imprinting is activated. Instead of the date, it is possible to imprint the day and time in 24-hour notation. The number for the day always precedes the time. Instead of the 24-hour notation it is also possible to use the 12-hour clock, with a for

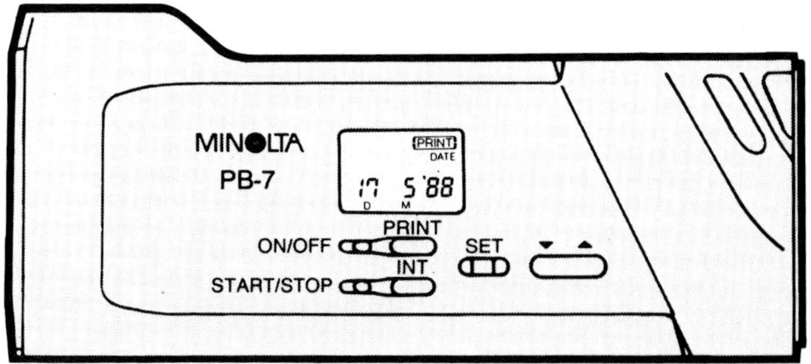

The Program Back PB7 enables the imprinting of data onto the film, control of long exposures, and the setting-up of interval sequences

Data imprint

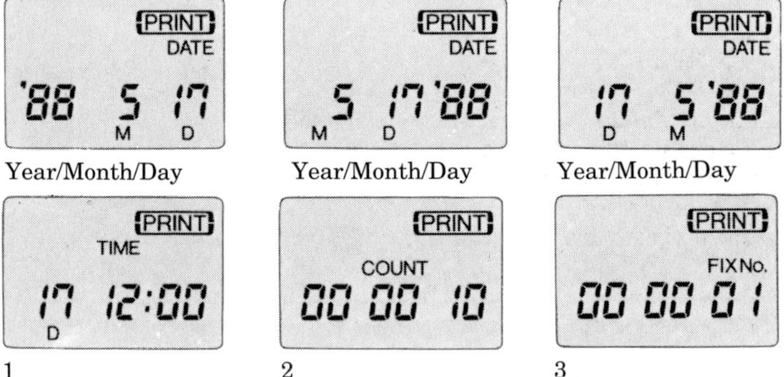

(1) day and time in 24-hour notation – (2) six-digit number; increasing after each exposure by one – (3) six digit code that does not change from one exposures to the next.

Interval function

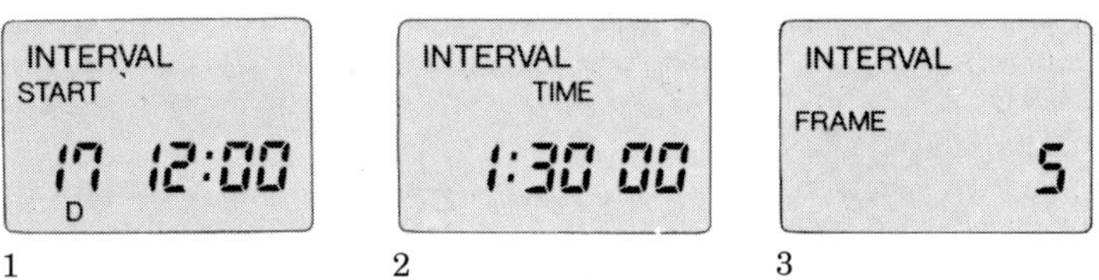

1 2 3

(1) starting time: day, hour and minute of the first shot – (2) interval: length of this can be up to 99 hours 59 minutes 59 seconds – (3) number of exposures: this can be any number from 1 to 99.

Long exposures

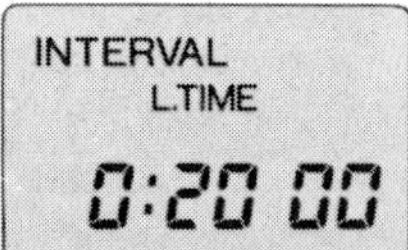

The exposure may be any time between 1 second and 9 hours 59 minutes 59 seconds.

Data imprint with Data Back DB-7

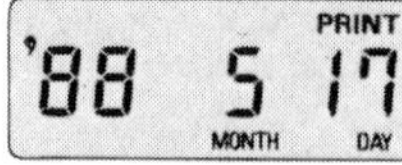

Year/Month/Day

Year/Month/Day

Year/Month/Day

Day and time

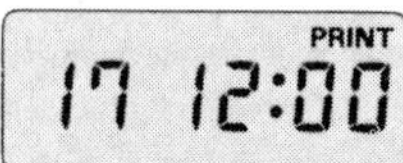

Day and time, 24hr clock

Time, 12hr clock

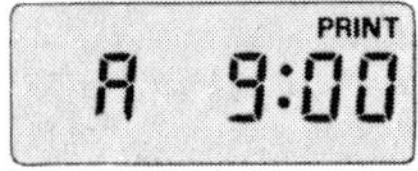

1

2

3

(1) a.m. • (2) p.m. • (3) Imprint of data can be switched off at any time.

a.m. and p for p.m. If the data imprinting facility is switched off, the display confirms this by displaying **OFF** in the LCD panel. Programming is done by using the **MODE SELECT** and **ADJUST** buttons. The type of imprinting data to be modified, i.e. the date, or day and time in 12-hour notation, or no-data imprinting, is via the **SELECT** button and the actual modifications are via the **ADJUST** button. The imprinted data appear at the bottom right of the frame.

Focusing Screens

The Minolta Dynax 8000i is fitted with the standard (Type G) Focusing Screen 7. This is a particularly bright focusing screen with markings indicating the large AF focus area as well as the centre focus area. It also has the small circle which indicates the area for spot metering. Two other screens are available and tweezers are supplied with them to enable quick, simple replacement by the user.

Focusing Screen Type L: This focusing screen has the same markings for the large and small AF focusing areas and a spot-metering circle. In addition, it is marked with a regular grid on a matt field. This screen is particularly useful for architectural photography or copying, when vertical and horizontal lines have to be precisely aligned. It is also very useful in revealing converging verticals when shooting with wide-angle lenses.

Focusing Screen Type S: Apart from the standard markings of the AF centre focus area, large focus area and spot metering circle, this focusing screen has vertical and horizontal scales on a matt field which are useful for macro, micro, and astronomical photography.

Eyepiece Corrector 1000

Although the Dynax 8000i sets the focus automatically, photographers who wear spectacles often have problems with assessing the picture through the viewfinder. For this reason Minolta offer nine eyepiece correction lenses with values between -4 and +3 dioptres for the Dynax 8000i. These lenses snap into the camera's eyepiece.

Viewfinder Magnifier Vn and Anglefinder Vn

Viewfinder Magnifier Vn enlarges the central viewfinder section 2.3-times and is particularly useful when using manual focus for macro shots with the camera on a tripod. The magnifier may be folded up to enable the whole of the frame to be viewed.

Anglefinder Vn can be used for viewing from above, below, or either side of the camera. The image remains laterally correct in any position. It is also indispensable when using the camera on a copying stand. For exact assessment of the viewing area it also offers 2-times magnification of the central section.

Macro Flash 1200 AF Set-N

A very useful and even essential accessory for flash photography in the close range. The Macro Flash 1200 AF (Set N) is technically identical to the Macro Flash 1200 AF, which is available for the Minolta 7000, but includes Flash Shoe Adapter FS-1100 to enable it to be fitted to Dynax models. Its advantage, apart from fully-automatic TTL flash control, is its extremely compact construction. The four flash tubes, arranged in a square around the optical axis, can be switched on and off individually, enabling you to illuminate the subject in different ways. The flash consists of two main components: The flash head and the control unit, the latter being attached to the accessory shoe of the Dynax 8000i via the Flash Shoe Adapter FS-1100, just like any other flashgun. The flash head is attached by a special adapter ring to the filter thread of the 50mm,f/2.8 or the 100mm,f/2.8 macro lenses. The flash head can be moved around the lens for best possible illumination.

To assist focusing there is a focusing lamp at each corner of the flash head. These also help to decide on the correct framing if the lighting conditions are poor. They are automatically extinguished when the release is lightly pressed or has not been touched for 30 sec. During the actual exposure they are switched off and they can also be switched off manually by a button at the rear of the control unit.

Automatic flash metering is controlled by the TTL flash control of the Dynax 8000i. Flash-ready and correct flash illumination are displayed in the viewfinder. In addition, flash-ready and confirma-

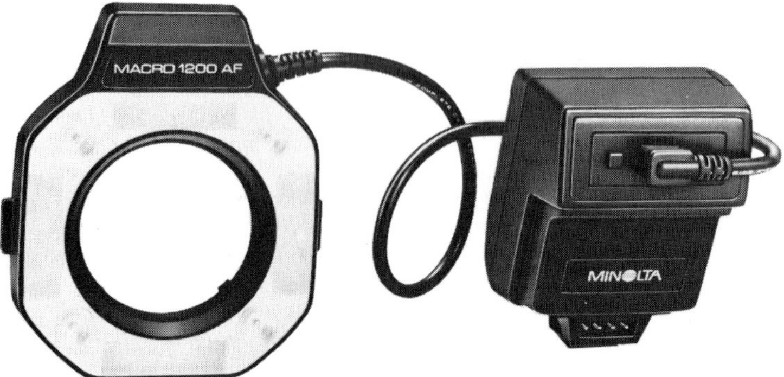

The Macro Flash 1200 AF Set-N consists of four individual flash tubes and four modelling lights. This unit is ideal in achieving a variety of illumination effects.

tion that the flash illumination was sufficient, are displayed on the back of the control unit. The correct aperture settings for various reproduction ratios may be read off the table at the back of the control unit.

The Macro Flash 1200 AF (Set-N) has a guide number of 12 at ISO 100/21° with all four flash tubes switched on. The power supply is by four 1.5v AA-size or appropriate rechargeable batteries. For continuous operation there is a power unit that can be plugged directly into the mains.

To save energy, the flash will automatically switch itself off if the release has not been activated after about one minute. Recharging begins as soon as the release is pressed. For interval sequences with Program Back PB-7 the flash is automatically charged about one minute before the programmed point of triggering the release.

Remote Cord RC-1000L and RC-1000S

Instead of the conventional wire release the Dynax 8000i uses a remote release which responds to electrical impulses. To use this facility you will need Remote Cord RC-1000L (5m) or RC-1000S (50cm). Both have a push button to activate the release. The cable is attached to the camera via a three-pin plug, the terminal is concealed behind a cover below the card door. The little cover can be kept safe in the cut-out of the hand unit of the release cable. A remote release cable may be needed to prevent camera shake for long exposures or macro shots from a tripod. Pressing the release switch in the hand unit in the release cable will activate both the autofocus system and the exposure metering of the Dynax 8000i. The remote release functions according to the same principle as the release on the camera itself, the only difference being that it also has a catch for keeping the shutter open in BULB setting. When the release is in this position a red marker becomes visible, indicating that the shutter is locked open. To close the shutter, the release button has to be unlocked. Take care that the red marker is not visible when attaching the cable, otherwise the shutter will be released.

Wireless Controller IR-1N Set

It is also possible to trigger the shutter release of the Dynax 8000i by a wireless remote control. To do this you will need Wireless Controller IR-1N Set. This unit is identical to the Wireless Controller of the Minolta 7000. Since the receiver unit cannot be attached directly to the Dynax accessory shoe, it should be connected to the bracket supplied with the IR-IN Set which fits between the camera and tripod. Alternately, Flash Shoe Adapter FS-1100 can be used. In addition, the receiver has to be connected with a cable to the remote release socket.

The transmitter and the receiver each have three channels, allowing the simultaneous control of any number of cameras in up to three individual groups, provided each camera is fitted with a receiver. This type of remote release is necessary if larger distances have to be bridged, or if it is impracticable to have too many trailing cables between the various units. The camera must be prefocused, either manually or automatically, since the autofocus mechanism cannot be triggered by the infrared release.

Filters and other Lens Attachments

Minolta offers different types of filters for black-and-white and colour photography which require the photographer to know certain basic rules as to their handling and effect. Further attachments for Minolta AF lenses are the achromatic close-up lenses to decrease the close-up distance, as well as the often underestimated lens hood.

UV Filter: Film emulsions tend to react strongly to UV radiation with heavy blue hues and a loss in sharpness. Strong UV radiation is often found in mountains and on the sea. However, UV-absorbing filters are completely colourless and absorb no light, so they do not influence the exposure in any way, and they are often kept on the lens to protect the front element.

Skylight Filter 1B/1A: These filters produce a slightly warmer colour rendering. They suppress blue for subjects in so-called open shade without direct sunlight which reflect the blue of the sky. They also result in warmer colours in dull and hazy conditions. The 1B filter has a slightly stronger effect than the 1A.

Conversion filters: These are used to adjust the colour value of colour film for the temperature of the illumination. Filter type B12 (blue) is used to suppress the red bias, when using daylight film with tungsten light. Filter R12 (red) is used when a tungsten film is used in daylight; in this case the heavy blue hue is suppressed.

Polarising Filter: These remove reflections from non-metallic surfaces at certain angles. A shot taken with a polarising filter usually has stronger colours and the sky is a deeper blue. The effect of the filter can be varied by turning it and checking the effect on the focusing screen. The strongest effect on a blue sky is at a 90o position of the shooting direction in the direction of the sun's rays. There is one problem when using polarising filters on an AF lens. The front barrel of some lenses rotates during focusing, which means that the polarising filter is turned as well. The filter therefore has to be adjusted after correct focus has been set. It may be better to change to manual focusing when using a polarising filter. There are also filter holders available which enable the front element to move freely.

The autofocus system and the exposure metering of the Minolta 8000i will only allow circular polarising filters to be used. The linear polarising filters affect the AF and exposure metering of the camera and are not recommended.

Neutral Density Filter ND-4X: These special filters are neutral grey and do not affect the colour rendering. They are used in colour and black-and-white photography if the light is too bright, or to enable the use of large apertures or slower shutter speeds in bright conditions to achieve special effects.

Filters for B&W Photography: Minolta offers four filters of this type - yellow, green, orange and red. Yellow improves the reproduction of blue sky and clouds. Green also darkens blue sky and lightens the greens of grass and foliage. Orange is often used for landscapes. They produce dark dramatic skies.

Red filters have a similar but even more intense effect: the blue of the sky appears very dark. Red filters are also used for infrared photography. The high density of some red filters could affect the AF system of the Dynax but you should experience no problem with the Minolta R60 filter. Since all colour filters absorb light to varying degrees, the exposure must be increased to compensate for this. However, this is automatically taken into account by the TTL exposure control of the Dynax 8000i.

Gelatin Filter Holders: Kodak offers 7.5x7.5cm light-balancing filters. These adjust the colour temperature of the illumination to the colour sensitivity of the film emulsion and are clamped in special Minolta filter holders, which are screwed into the filter thread of the lens.

Minolta Portrayer Filters: As the word "Portrayer" may already suggest, these are soft-focus effect filters used for portrait photography. The Minolta ones are available in two types, with different effects. S1 and S2, supplied as a set, are intended for general soft-focus photography with lenses of focal length between 50mm and 210mm and P1, P2, P3, available as a set, are for particularly flattering portraits. This filter type has a special softening effect on skin tones. They are distinct from other filters of this type because the aperture value does not affect the softening effect; the focal length of the lens, on the other hand, does play an important role. This makes these filters particularly useful in program mode, when the aperture cannot be controlled manually. The soft-focus effect increases with increasing focal length. If a strong soft-focus effect is desired, more than one filter can be used. All these Portrayer filters depict the centre in sharp focus, with the soft-focus effect increasing towards the edge of the frame.

Achromatic Close-up Lenses: These are used to decrease the close focusing distance and thereby increase the reproduction ratio. The Minolta type consist of two cemented elements which are screwed into the filter thread of the lens. Compared with simple close-up lenses, achromatic lenses give a much better quality of reproduction. At f/8 and smaller, reproduction quality is very acceptable - larger apertures are not recommended.

Minolta offers three lenses with different powers which can be combined to obtain different reproduction ratios. Always attach the close-up lens with the smaller number first. The autofocus system is not adversely affected through the use of these attachments. However, it is important to stay within the restricted distance range within which focusing is still possible.

They are available in 49 and 55mm filter thread sizes. They are identified as 0 for +0.94 dioptres, 1 for +2.0 dioptres and 2 for +3.8 dioptres.

Lens Hood: This is a very useful and almost indispensable accessory. With some Minolta lenses the hood is already built-in, but others are supplied with a separate clip-on or bayonet-fitting hood. They prevent light entering the lens from an oblique angle, which can refract differently and scatter inside the lens. The effect is poor contrast and an impression of unsharpness. Lens hoods are another means of ensuring good quality pictures and are a simple, relatively cheap and often underestimated accessory.